Houghton
Mifflin
Harcourt

Writing

Grade 2

ISBN 978-0-5442-6846-3

2 3 4 5 6 7 8 9 10   0982   22 21 20 19 18 17 16 15 14

4500510529   A B C D E F G

Core Skills Writing

GRADE 2

Table of Contents

Introduction iv
Features v
Skills Correlation vi
Writing Rubric viii

Unit 1: Laying the Foundation

Writing and Talking 1
Journal Writing 2
Forms of Writing 3
A Reason to Write 4
The Reader 5
Nouns 6
Special Nouns 7
Pronouns 8
Verbs 9
Verbs—Then and Now 10
Adjectives 11
The Writing Process: Prewriting 12
The Writing Process: Drafting 13
The Writing Process: Revising 14
The Writing Process: Proofreading 15
The Writing Process: Publishing 16
Writing Trait: Ideas 17
Writing Trait: Grouping Ideas and Details 18
Writing Trait: Voice 19
Writing Trait: Words 20
Writing Trait: Sentences 21
Writing Trait: Proofreading 22
Writing Trait: Sharing 23
What to Write? 24

Unit 2: Building Sentences

What Is a Sentence? 25
Sentence Order 26
Sentence Parts 27
Present Tense Verbs 28
Past Tense Verbs 29
Telling Sentences 30
Asking Sentences 31
Exclamations 32
Exact Nouns 33
Lively Verbs 34
Add Adjectives 35
The Reader's Senses 36
Words That Paint a Picture 37
Synonyms 38
Antonyms 39
Homophones 40
Joining Sentences with the Same Naming Part 41
Joining Sentences with the Same Action Part 42
Joining Sentences to List Words 43
Sentence Length 44
Sentence Beginnings 45
Run-on Sentences 46
Proofreading Sentences 47
Self-Assessment: Sentences 48

Unit 3: Building Paragraphs

What Is a Paragraph? 50
Parts of a Paragraph 51
Paragraph Order 52
The Right Size Paragraph 53
Drawing a Picture 54
Listing What You Need to Know 55
Writing a Topic Sentence 56

© Houghton Mifflin Harcourt Publishing Company

Writing Detail Sentences 57

Writing an Ending Sentence 58

Starting to Write 59

Keeping to the Topic 60

Paragraphs That Flow 61

Time-Order Words 62

Writing Pattern: Main Idea and Details 63

Writing Pattern: Sequence of Events 64

Writing Pattern: Compare and Contrast 65

Writing Pattern: Problem and Solution 66

Writing Pattern: Cause and Effect 67

Writing Pattern: Summary 68

Adding Details 69

Choosing a Title 70

Self-Assessment: Paragraphs 71

Unit 4: Writing Forms

Personal Story 73

Person Description 75

Place Description 77

Thing Description 79

How-to Paragraph 81

Information Paragraph 83

Compare and Contrast Paragraph 85

Rhyme 87

Poem 89

Friendly Letter 91

Invitation 93

Observation Log 95

Opinion Paragraph 97

Book Report 99

Short Story 101

Research Report 105

Blackline Masters

Journal Paper 109

The Writing Process 110

Prewriting Survey 112

Proofreading Checklist 115

Proofreading Marks 116

Writing Traits Checklist 117

Writing Interest Survey 119

Main Idea and Details Web 121

Sequence Chart 122

Venn Diagram 123

Problem and Solution Chart 124

Cause and Effect Charts 125

Summary Chart 126

Answer Key 127

Introduction

Writing is one of the core skills necessary for success in school and in life. Good writers can communicate effectively with others. Good writing is a skill acquired through guidance, practice, and self-evaluation. This book provides guidance for success in different writing formats. This book also provides many opportunities for writing practice. Finally, this book encourages writers to examine their own work, as well as that of their peers, and judge its qualities and flaws.

Clear writing and clear speaking are products of clear thinking. Clear thinking is a product of good organization of ideas. Good organization is a product of careful planning. One good way to plan is through graphic organizers.

- In this book, different kinds of graphic organizers are provided for students to plan their writing.

- One kind of graphic organizer, emphasized in Unit 2, allows writers to "see" their writing clearly.

- By "seeing" their writing, students can more easily determine how the different parts of a sentence work together to produce a clear expression of their main idea.

- This kind of graphic organizer allows students a more visual and tactile appreciation of their writing. It also appeals to multiple intelligences.

Organization

This book is divided into four units. Each unit builds upon earlier units. Using this scaffolded approach, students will find that writing becomes like construction.

- **Unit 1: Laying the Foundation** addresses basic concepts of writing, such as good writing traits and the process of writing.

- **Unit 2: Building Sentences** emphasizes the act of writing. Writers first deal with the main idea of a sentence and then expand sentences by adding other parts of speech.

- **Unit 3: Building Paragraphs** focuses on the structure and content of a well-written paragraph. Writers also learn about revising, proofreading, publishing, and self- and peer-evaluation in this unit.

- **Unit 4: Writing Forms** provides guidance and practice writing in different formats such as narration, description, persuasion, opinion, and short stories.

Write Away

For too many students, writing is a struggle or a pain. They may not realize the benefits of being a good writer, or they may not care. This book tries to reach out to all writers with a light tone and an approach that allows students to "see" their writing in a new light. Writing does not have to be a chore. It can be fun. Students just have to be reminded that good writing can be their golden ticket to success in school and life.

Features

The title clearly identifies the skill. identifies the skill.

Examples model the skill.

Bullets highlight important points of the skill.

Students creatively apply the skill in **WRITE AWAY.**

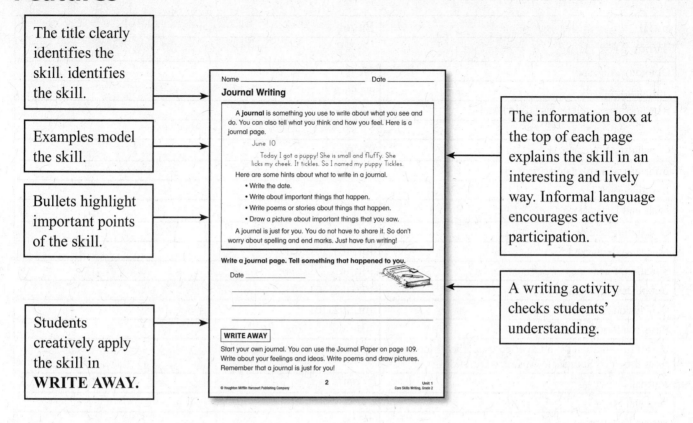

The information box at the top of each page explains the skill in an interesting and lively way. Informal language encourages active participation.

A writing activity checks students' understanding.

Checklists guide students through the writing process.

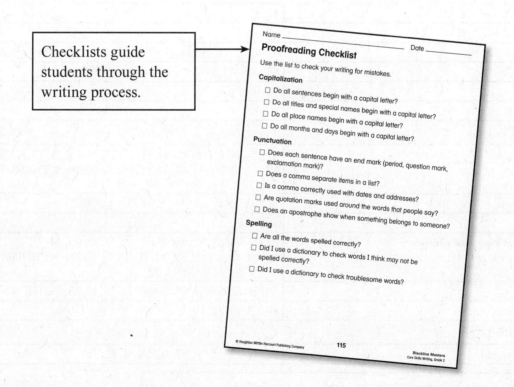

Skills Correlation

Skill	Page
Types of Writing	
Opinion Paragraph *	97, 98
Introduction *	97, 98
Reasons Supported by Facts and Details *	97, 98
Linking Words *	97, 98
Concluding Statement or Section *	97, 98
Informative/Explanatory Texts *	83, 84
Introduction *	83
Facts and Definitions *	83
Concluding Statement or Section *	58, 83
Narrative Paragraph *	101, 102, 103, 104
Situation, Event Sequence *	101, 102, 103, 104
Detail Development *	101, 102, 103, 104
Conclusion *	101, 102, 104
Research Report *	105, 106, 107, 108
Recall Information from Experiences/Gather Information from Provided Sources to Answer a Question	105, 106, 107, 108
Journal	2, 109
Personal Story	73, 74
Person Description	75, 76
Place Description	77, 78
Thing Description	79, 80
How-to Paragraph	81, 82
Compare and Contrast Paragraph	85, 86
Rhyme	87, 88
Poem	89, 90
Friendly Letter	91, 92
Invitation	93, 94
Observation Log	95, 96
Book Report	99, 100
Writing Process	
Development and Organization *	12, 13, 14, 15, 16, 48, 49, 71, 72, 73, 74, 75, 76, 77, 78, 79, 80, 81, 82, 83, 84, 85, 86, 87, 88, 89, 90, 91, 92, 93, 94, 95, 96, 97, 98, 99, 100, 101, 102, 103, 104, 105, 106, 107, 108, 110
Audience	5, 111
Voice	19
Planning, Revising, and Editing *	12, 13, 14, 15, 22, 48, 49, 59, 69, 71, 72, 73, 74, 75, 76, 77, 78, 79, 80, 81, 82, 83, 84, 85, 86, 89, 90, 91, 92, 93, 94, 95, 96, 100, 101, 102, 103, 110, 111, 112
Topic	24, 51, 52, 53, 54, 55, 56, 60, 71, 72, 81, 83, 89, 111, 112
Publishing/Publishing Using Technology *	16, 23, 49, 72, 110
Composition	
Paragraph Structure	50, 51, 52, 53, 56, 57, 58, 60, 61, 62

*Aligns with Grade 2 Common Core State Standards for English Language Arts

Skills Correlation, part 2

Skill	Page
Vocabulary	
Synonyms	38
Antonyms	39
Homophones	40
Sentences	
Recognizing Sentences and Sentence Types*	25, 26, 27, 30, 31, 32
Subjects and Predicates*	27, 41, 42, 43, 47
Combining Sentences*	41, 42, 43
Expanding Sentences*	33, 35
Run-on Sentences	46
Grammar and Usage	
Nouns	6, 7, 8, 22, 28, 33, 45, 67
Verbs*	9, 10, 28, 29, 34, 67, 74, 80
Pronouns	8, 45, 73
Adjectives	11, 35, 36, 38, 75, 76, 77, 78, 79, 80
Capitalization and Punctuation	
Capitalization: First Word in Sentence	22, 25, 26, 30, 31, 32, 47, 113
Capitalization: Proper Nouns*	7, 22, 113
Capitalization: Abbreviations and Titles	7, 22, 113
End Punctuation	22, 25, 26, 30, 31, 32, 46, 47, 113
Commas*	43, 91, 113

*Aligns with Grade 2 Common Core State Standards for English Language Arts

Writing Rubric

Score of 4
The student:

- clearly and completely addresses the writing task,
- demonstrates an understanding of the purpose for writing,
- maintains a single focus,
- presents a main idea supported by relevant details,
- uses paragraphs to organize main ideas and supporting ideas under the umbrella of a thesis statement,
- presents content in a logical order and sequence and uses transitions effectively,
- uses variety in sentence types, beginnings, and lengths,
- chooses the correct writing pattern and form to communicate ideas clearly,
- clearly portrays feelings through voice and word choice,
- uses language appropriate to the writing task, such as language rich in sensory details in a descriptive passage,
- uses vocabulary to suit purpose and audience,
- summarizes main ideas in a concluding paragraph when appropriate,
- establishes and defends a position in a persuasive paragraph, and
- has few or no errors in the standard rules of English grammar, punctuation, capitalization, and spelling.

Score of 3
The student:

- generally follows the criteria described above, and
- has some errors in the standard rules of English grammar, punctuation, capitalization, and spelling, but not enough to impair a reader's comprehension.

Score of 2
The student:

- marginally follows the criteria described above, and
- has several errors in the standard rules of English grammar, punctuation, capitalization, and spelling that may impair a reader's comprehension.

Score of 1
The student:

- fails to follow the criteria described above, and
- has many errors in the standard rules of English grammar, punctuation, capitalization, and spelling that impair a reader's comprehension.

Writing and Talking

Do you like to write? Some students do not. They like to tell their ideas. But writing is like talking. You use words when you talk, and you use words when you write.

Sometimes it is better to write than to talk. You can think about your ideas. You can plan what you want to write. When you talk, you might not think first. Something you didn't mean to say could pop out of your mouth! You might not clearly explain your idea, either.

Write a word from the box to complete each sentence.

think   clearly   words

1. You use _____ when you write and talk.

2. When you write, you can _____ about your ideas.

3. When you write, you can explain your ideas _____.

WRITE AWAY

Do you like to write? Tell why or why not.

_____

_____

_____

_____

1

Name _____ Date _____

Journal Writing

A **journal** is something you use to write about what you see and do. You can also tell what you think and how you feel. Here is a journal page.

June 10

Today I got a puppy! She is small and fluffy. She licks my cheek. It tickles. So I named my puppy Tickles.

Here are some hints about what to write in a journal.

- Write the date.
- Write about important things that happen.
- Write poems or stories about things that happen.
- Draw a picture about important things that you saw.

A journal is just for you. You do not have to share it. So don't worry about spelling and end marks. Just have fun writing!

Write a journal page. Tell something that happened to you.

Date _____

_____

_____

_____

WRITE AWAY

Start your own journal. You can use the Journal Paper on page 109. Write about your feelings and ideas. Write poems and draw pictures. Remember that a journal is just for you!

2

Forms of Writing

A journal is just one kind, or **form**, of writing. There are many other forms of writing, too.

- A **letter** is a message sent to someone.
- A **poster** is a large paper with information telling important facts.
- An **ad** gives information about something you can buy.
- A **list** is quickly written words and ideas that have something alike.

Just look around you. You can probably see many different forms of writing. How do you know what kind each is? How do you know a letter when you see it? How do you know a story when you see it? You know because each form has a special look. The ideas are often organized in a special way, too. They are written in a certain order and pattern.

How many different forms of writing can you think of? Try to write at least six.

_____ _____ _____

_____ _____ _____

WRITE AWAY

What kind of writing do you like to do? Get a sheet of paper. Tell about your favorite form of writing. Then tell why you like this kind of writing.

3

A Reason to Write

Think about the last time you wrote something. Did you write a letter? Did you write answers to science questions? Did you write a funny story? No matter what kind of writing it was, you had a reason to write. You had a **purpose** for putting the words on the paper.

Writers have four purposes for writing.

A. They want to share their feelings or ideas.

B. They want to make people laugh, cry, or get angry.

C. They want to get others to think or act a certain way.

D. They want to tell information.

You need to think about your purpose for writing. It will help you choose the form of writing you will use.

Look at each kind of writing. What is the purpose?
Write the letter for the purpose on the line.

1. a report about sharks _____

2. a speech about helping whales _____

3. an invitation to a party _____

4. a poem about a frog that cannot hop _____

WRITE AWAY

Imagine that a butterfly landed on your nose. You want to write about it. What is your purpose? What form of writing would you use? Answer the questions on a sheet of paper. Tell why you think as you do.

4

Name _____ Date _____

The Reader

Imagine that you just wrote a story. What will you do with it? Most likely, you will ask people to read it. You will give your story to an **audience** who will want to read it. The audience will be the ones reading or listening to your work.

Writers choose a form of writing to match the audience. Here are some questions to help you think about the audience.

- Who will read what I write?
- What will the reader want to read?
- What words will the reader understand?

Read the audience names. Then look at the pictures. Who will read each form of writing? Write the name on the line.

child   adult   teen

1.

_____

2.

_____

3.

_____

WRITE AWAY

Think of a time you did something special. Imagine writing a letter to a grandparent telling him or her about it. Now imagine writing a letter to a four-year-old child. Would you use the same words? Why or why not? Tell your ideas on a sheet of paper.

Nouns

We say and write words to share our thoughts and feelings. Each word belongs to a special group, or part of speech. One of the most important parts of speech is a **noun.** A noun is a word that names a person, place, or thing.

My **uncle** is tall.   (person)

The **zoo** is closed.   (place)

The **bird** can sing.   (thing)

Look at each picture. Write if it is a <u>person</u>, <u>place</u>, or <u>thing</u>.

1.

   _____

2.

   _____

3.

   _____

WRITE AWAY

On a sheet of paper, write the name of one person, place, and thing. Then draw a picture that shows each item. Below the picture, write words that tell what is happening in the picture.

Special Nouns

What is your name? What street do you live on? The answers are nouns, but they are special nouns.

Remember that a noun is a word that names a person, place, or thing. Some nouns are special. They name certain people, places, and things. All special nouns begin with a capital letter.

Ellen walks her turtle.   (special person)

They go to **Pink Palace Park.**   (special place)

They ride the **Curvy Wormy Roller Coaster.**   (special thing)

Here are more special nouns. They begin with a capital letter, too.

- titles of people (**Mr.** Magoo, **Dr.** Bandage)
- days of the week, months, and holidays (**Saturday, July, Fourth of July**)

Answer the questions.

1. What is the name of your street? _____

2. What is your neighbor's name? _____

3. What is your favorite day? _____

4. What is your favorite month? _____

WRITE AWAY

What do you like to do on Saturday morning? On a sheet of paper, draw a picture of yourself doing the action. Write words that tell what is happening in the picture. Try to write at least two special nouns.

Pronouns

You just learned about nouns. A noun is a word that names a person, place, or thing. Now you will learn about a **pronoun.** A pronoun can take the place of a noun. You use pronouns so that you will not repeat words.

Sentences with Nouns	**Sentences with Pronouns**
Ed fell in the mud puddle.	**He** fell into the mud puddle.
The mud made a mess.	**It** made a mess.
Jan and Cindy hosed off the mud.	**They** hosed off the mud.

Here are pronouns.

    I   you   he   she   it   we   they

Look at each picture. Write a noun that names it. Then write a pronoun that could take the place of each noun.

1.

2.

3.

_____

_____

WRITE AWAY

Go on a pronoun hunt! Look through a book. On a sheet of paper, write five pronouns you see. Then write the noun that each pronoun names.

Verbs

A **verb** is another important part of speech. A verb shows action. It can also tell about being. All sentences have verbs.

The snake **slides** across the road.   (action verb)

The snake **is** green.   (being verb)

Look at each picture. Write a verb to match it.

1.

_____

2.

_____

3.

_____

WRITE AWAY

Write a sentence using each verb above.

_____

_____

_____

_____

_____

Verbs—Then and Now

A **verb** shows action and tells about being. A verb also tells when something is happening. Verbs can tell about something happening now or in the past.

Lance **calls** the bear.   (happening now)

Lance **called** the bear last week.   (happened in the past)

Look at the picture. Follow the directions.

1. Write words to tell that the action is happening now.

_____

2. Write words to tell that the action happened yesterday.

_____

WRITE AWAY

Write a sentence to tell something you are doing now. Write another sentence to tell what you did yesterday.

_____

_____

Adjectives

An **adjective** is another part of speech. It describes a noun. It tells how something looks, feels, tastes, sounds, or smells. It also tells how many. Writers like to use adjectives. Adjectives help readers picture what a writer is saying.

One little green grasshopper played an **old wooden** violin.

Color the picture. Write an adjective in front of each noun to tell about your picture.

1. _____ slide

2. _____ children

3. _____ hair

WRITE AWAY

On a sheet of paper, draw a picture. You can use a pencil, markers, or crayons. Then write adjectives to describe your picture.

11

The Writing Process: Prewriting

Sometimes you might have trouble deciding what you should write. There are steps that you can follow to help you write something special. The steps are called the **writing process.**

Prewriting is the first step. This is where you plan your writing. Here is what you do when you prewrite.

- Plan what you will write.

- List ideas or make a web.

- Think about who will read the work.

- Think about what writing form to use.

Follow the directions.

1. What is your favorite carnival ride? List three ideas.

   Idea 1

   Idea 2 _____

   Idea 3

2. Choose one idea. Write it on a sheet of paper. Then write adjectives that tell how the ride looks, smells, feels, tastes, and sounds.

WRITE AWAY

Use the Prewriting Survey on pages 111–112 to guide you through the prewriting steps. Make a plan of what to write.

The Writing Process: Drafting

When you write, you follow the steps in the writing process. The steps will help you do your best writing. You know about the first step of prewriting. **Drafting** is the second step. Here is what you do when you write a draft.

- Put your ideas into words and sentences.
- Don't worry about mistakes. You will fix them later!

Look on page 12. Read your prewriting ideas about the carnival ride. Practice drafting. Tell what the ride looks like.

_____

_____

_____

_____

WRITE AWAY

On a sheet of paper, finish the draft that tells about the carnival ride. Use the writing form you chose on the Prewriting Survey. Use words that your audience will understand.

The Writing Process: Revising

You are learning about the writing process. The writing process has five steps. The steps help you do your best writing. You have practiced prewriting and drafting. Now you will learn about the third step, which is **revising.** Here is what you do when you revise.

- Read your sentences, or have a partner read your sentences.
- Make sure the ideas are easy to understand.
- Add or remove information so the writing makes sense.
- Move ideas around so they are in order.
- Make a clean copy of your work.

Have a partner read your draft about the carnival ride. Ask your partner if the draft makes sense. Ask him or her for ideas to make your draft better. Then write two changes that would make it better.

_____

_____

_____

_____

WRITE AWAY

On a sheet of paper, write a clean copy of the carnival ride story. Make the changes you wrote above. Fix other problems you see.

The Writing Process: Proofreading

The writing process has five steps to help you do your best writing. You have learned about three of the steps. Now it is time to learn about the fourth step. It is **proofreading.** You can proofread your own writing. You can also ask a partner to proofread your writing.

When you proofread, you read your writing three times. You look for a special kind of mistake each time.

- Read once to make sure that words beginning with a capital letter are correct.

- Read a second time to make sure all the end marks are correct.

- Read a third time to make sure all words are spelled correctly.

You can use the Proofreading Checklist on page 113 to help you remember what to look for. You can use the Proofreading Marks on page 114. **Proofreading marks** are special signs that show you where the mistakes are.

Read the paragraph. Fix the mistakes using the Proofreading Marks on page 114. (Hint: There are four mistakes.)

Hoppy the Frog did not like to hop. He liked to run. then one day, Slide the Snake got close to Hoppy. Hoppy ran, but slide stayed right beside him. Then, Hoppy hopped. Slide culd not hop. Hoppy got away Hoppy decided that he liked to hop after all!

WRITE AWAY

Ask a partner to proofread your carnival ride story. Tell your partner to use the Proofreading Checklist and Proofreading Marks.

The Writing Process: Publishing

The fifth step in the writing process is **publishing.** There are many ways to publish your writing. You can write it neatly. You can type it on a computer. Here is what you do in this step.

- Write or type your final draft.

- Give your writing a title. Put your name on your writing.

- Think of ways to share your writing. Will you read it aloud? Will you publish it as part of a class blog?

- Add pictures or charts to your writing. You can draw them yourself. You can also find them on a computer.

Blog is short for "weblog." It is a journal that you keep on the Internet. Others can read and comment on your writing. Here are the important parts of a blog.

Blog Part	Example
• URL, or web address	• http://www._____.com/blog
• Blog name	• Mrs. Romo's Second Grade Class Blog
• Post title	• Carnival Ride Stories
• Byline (who wrote the post and when)	• by Joan on May 11 at 2:30 p.m.
• Blog post	• [Insert your writing]
• Comments	• Name of reader leaving comment, followed by the comment.

With your teacher's help, plan a class blog on a sheet of paper.

Writing Trait: Ideas

Now that you know the steps for writing, it's time to look at ways to make your writing clear. There are seven traits, or skills, that can help you. You will learn about these **writing traits** in the next several pages. You can also see all the traits listed on pages 115–116.

One trait has to do with your **ideas.** Ideas are the thoughts and pictures you form in your mind. When you write, you want readers to understand your thoughts.

Here are some hints to help you choose the best ideas to write about.

- Tell about one important idea. It is the **main idea.**
- Choose a main idea that is interesting.
- Add **details.** Details are the facts that tell more about your main idea.
- Details tell what you see, hear, smell, taste, and feel.

Look at the picture. Then answer the questions on a sheet of paper.

1. What is the main idea?

2. What are three details you see?

WRITE AWAY

On a sheet of paper, write about the picture above. Tell the main idea and the details.

Writing Trait: Grouping Ideas and Details

Writing traits are skills that you can use to make your writing better. One trait is called **organization.** Organization is the way that you group ideas and details. You should group your ideas in a way that makes sense. Then your message will be clear.

Here are some hints to help you organize your writing.

- Choose a writing form that makes the information clear. (Letters, e-mail messages, stories, and journals are some writing forms that you can choose.)

- Show a beginning, a middle, and an end.

- Write the first sentence so that it catches the reader's interest.

- Put details in order.

- Use clue words to show the order (first, next, then, finally, after that, at the same time).

Look at the pictures. Then write numbers I through 3 to show how you would order them.

_____   _____   _____

WRITE AWAY

On a sheet of paper, write a story about the pictures above. Use the hints to help you organize your writing.

Writing Trait: Voice

When you talk, you use your **voice.** Voice is the sound that comes out of your mouth. Your voice shows how you feel. When you are happy, you use a happy voice and happy words.

You can show your voice when you write, too. Use these hints to help you.

- Choose words that show your feelings.
- Choose words that your reader can understand.

Look at the picture. Then read the names of an audience. Tell about the picture in words that each reader can understand.

Grandfather _____

Two-year-old boy _____

WRITE AWAY

On a sheet of paper, draw a picture of something that makes you happy. Tell about the picture in two different ways. Write words that an adult can understand. Then write words that your best friend can understand.

Writing Trait: Words

What you think and feel is important. So you want a reader to understand what you write. The words you choose should help the reader get the exact picture. One writing trait is to choose words that will help your reader understand your ideas.

Here are some hints to help you choose the best words.

- Choose words that help a reader see, hear, taste, smell, and touch.
- Use strong action words to tell what is happening.
- Use exact words.
- Use new words.

Think about an apple. Write words to describe it.

What does it look like? _____

What does it smell like? _____

What does it feel like? _____

What does it taste like? _____

What does it sound like when you bite into it? _____

WRITE AWAY

Look out a window. What do you see? Choose one object. Write exact words that describe it. If it is moving, choose strong action words to tell how it moves.

_____

_____

Writing Trait: Sentences

A **sentence** is a group of words that tells a complete thought. When you talk, the sentences flow out one after the other. They are smooth, and they do not sound choppy.

The sentences you write should be the same way. When someone reads them, the sentences should sound like you are talking. One of the writing traits is to write smooth sentences.

Here are some hints to help you write smooth sentences.

- Write some sentences that are short and some that are long.
- Write sentences that begin with different kinds of words.
- Write sentences that sound like you are talking.

Read the sentences. Write them so they sound better. Change how they begin. Make some long and some short.

Amy has a duck. The duck is white. The duck has yellow feet. The duck likes to swim.

_____

_____

_____

_____

WRITE AWAY

Do you know the story "The Three Little Pigs"? On a sheet of paper, write the story. Use the hints for writing good sentences.

Writing Trait: Proofreading

When you write a draft, you do not worry about mistakes. But it is important to proofread your writing and correct the mistakes. If your writing has lots of mistakes, it will be hard for the reader to understand your ideas. So, one trait of good writing is to fix mistakes.

Here are some hints to help you proofread.

- Write a capital letter at the beginning of each sentence.
- Write an end mark at the end of each sentence.
- Write a capital letter at the beginning of each special noun.
- Spell all words correctly.
- Put a space between all words.

Read the paragraph. Fix the mistakes. Use the Proofreading Marks on page 114. (Hint: There are four mistakes.)

Elton has a dog named rolo. Elton took Rolo to

the park Rolo chased a squirrel. He chased a burd.

he did not chase the stick that Elton threw. By then,

Rolo was too tired!

WRITE AWAY

On a sheet of paper, write sentences telling what you like to do in the park. Make three mistakes in the writing. Then ask a friend or family member to find and fix the mistakes.

Writing Trait: Sharing

The writing trait of **sharing** is like the writing process step of publishing. You have worked really hard to write your ideas. So you want the reader to enjoy reading what you wrote. You can help your reader enjoy the work by making it look interesting.

Here are some hints to help you make your work ready to share.

- Write a title that will catch a reader's interest.
- Draw pictures to show the main ideas.
- Make the final copy clean and neat.
- Make a cover.

Look at each picture. Write a title that will catch a reader's interest.

_____   _____

WRITE AWAY

What is the title of your favorite book? Write the title below. Tell why it is a good title.

My favorite book is _____.

It is a good title because _____.

What to Write?

Most of the time, someone will tell you what to write. He or she will also tell you what form to use. You might have to answer questions, or you might have to write a letter. But what if you feel like writing on your own? What should you write about?

At times like this, you can write about something you really like. You can write about a **topic** that you know a lot about, too. The topic is what you know or write about. Most likely, you know lots of details and facts about the topic. So, you will have much to say.

What kinds of things interest you? What topics do you know about? Make a list of six of these.

_____

_____

_____

_____

_____

_____

WRITE AWAY

There is another way to choose what to write. You can answer the questions on the Writing Interest Survey. It is on pages 117–118. It will help you think about the kind of books you like to read. If you like a special kind of book, you just might like to try that form of writing!

What Is a Sentence?

A **sentence** is a group of words that tells a complete thought. Every sentence begins with a capital letter, and it ends with an end mark.

Birds fly.

Boys and girls play.

We like to laugh.

Are the words below sentences? Write <u>yes</u> or <u>no</u>.

1. Dancing. _____

2. Ant sings. _____

3. Cricket plays the guitar. _____

4. Two bees are in the band. _____

5. One big bug. _____

WRITE AWAY

Look at the words above. Which are not sentences? Add words to make them complete sentences.

_____

_____

_____

_____

Sentence Order

A **sentence** is a group of words that tells a complete thought. The words in a sentence must be in an order that makes sense.

Peanut butter is good.

We like juice.

Mr. Green eats lettuce.

Read each group of words. Use them to write a sentence that makes sense. Remember to write a capital letter at the beginning of each sentence. Write an end mark, too.

1. is fall it

_____

2. falling leaves are the

_____

3. Anna the rakes leaves

_____

4. is fun she having

_____

WRITE AWAY

Think of a sentence. Then cut a sheet of paper into cards. Write each word of the sentence on a different card. Ask a friend or family member to use the words to make a sentence that makes sense.

Sentence Parts

Every sentence has two parts. The **naming part** tells who or what the sentence is about.

The girls ride bikes.

Eric washes dishes.

The **action part** tells what someone or something does.

The girls **ride bikes.**

Eric **washes dishes.**

Every sentence needs a naming part and an action part to be a complete thought.

Write a word or words to complete each sentence.

I. _____ eats.

2. _____ reads.

3. Jill and Jan _____.

4. The bear _____.

WRITE AWAY

Write sentence parts below. Some should be a naming part. Some should be an action part. Ask a friend or family member to complete the sentences.

_____

_____

Present Tense Verbs

Some sentences tell about actions that are happening now. These sentences are written in the **present tense.** Add **s** to an action verb that tells about one person, place, or thing. You do not add an ending if the noun names more than one person, place, or thing.

The horse **runs.**   ←——   There is one horse, so add an **s** to the action verb.

The horses **run.**   ←——   There is more than one horse, so do not change the action verb.

Complete each sentence. Write a present tense action verb.

1. Three goats _____.

2. Flowers _____.

3. An elephant _____.

4. Keisha _____.

WRITE AWAY

Some nouns name one and more than one. One example is <u>sheep.</u> Write a sentence that uses the word to mean one sheep. Then write a sentence that uses the word to mean more than one sheep.

_____

_____

_____

Past Tense Verbs

Some sentences tell about actions that happened in the past. These sentences are written in the **past tense.** Most action verbs that are past tense end in **ed.** But some past tense verbs change. You will have to learn these action verbs.

Tran **sees** the train.   ⟵   The action happens now.

Tran **saw** the train last week.   ⟵   The action happened in the past.

Here are some other action verbs that change.

Now	Past
go, goes	went
come, comes	came
run, runs	ran
give, gives	gave

Write each sentence to show that the action happened in the past.

1. Ann goes to the park. _____

2. Sara comes with her. _____

3. They run to the swings. _____

WRITE AWAY

There are many other action verbs that change when they are past tense. Think of two more. Write them on a sheet of paper.

Telling Sentences

When you write, you want to hold the reader's interest. One way to make sure that the reader keeps reading is to write different kinds of sentences.

A **telling sentence** is one kind of sentence. It is the sentence that is used most often. A telling sentence is a group of words that tells something. Like all sentences, it begins with a capital letter. It ends with a **period (.)**.

My uncle lives on a farm**.**

Five sheep live on the farm, too**.**

The sheep eat corn**.**

Write three telling sentences about the picture.

1. _____

   _____

2. _____

   _____

3. _____

   _____

WRITE AWAY

On a sheet of paper, draw a picture of something. Write three clues about it. The clues should be telling sentences. Read the clues to a friend or family member. Ask the person to guess the picture.

Asking Sentences

An **asking sentence** is another kind of sentence. It is a group of words that asks a question. Each asking sentence begins with a capital letter. It ends with a **question mark (?).** Some of the words that begin a question are <u>who</u>, <u>what</u>, <u>where</u>, <u>when</u>, <u>why</u>, and <u>how</u>.

What is your favorite song**?**

Would you like oranges on your pizza**?**

Writers like to use questions in their work. Questions make a reader stop and think about the answer. Then the reader will want to keep on reading to find out what the writer has to say about the question.

Write three asking sentences that you could ask a firefighter.

1. _____

_____

_____

2. _____

_____

3. _____

_____

Exclamations

An **exclamation** adds zip to any writing. This kind of sentence is a group of words that shows strong feeling. Like other sentences, exclamations begin with a capital letter. They end with an **exclamation mark (!).**

What a big fish you caught!

Watch out for that snake!

Stop that dog!

Exclamations give the reader a clue that something exciting is happening. They might mean that you are excited about your idea. They can also mean that the action in the story is exciting. Using exclamations will keep the reader reading!

Look at the picture. Write three exclamations that you could say to the boy.

1. _____

_____

2. _____

_____

3. _____

_____

WRITE AWAY

Imagine that you are at the circus. On a sheet of paper, write five exclamations that you might say while you are watching the show.

32

Exact Nouns

You want to keep a reader interested in your writing. You also want a reader to understand exactly what you are saying. Using exact **nouns** will help you meet both goals. Exact nouns give more details.

Read this sentence.

She walked to the **park.**

Here is the same sentence written two different ways. Look at the exact nouns. They give more details.

Maya walked to **Oak Hill Park.**

The woman walked to the **picnic area.**

As a good writer, it is your job to make your sentences clear. Using exact nouns will help.

Write each sentence using exact nouns.

1. He went to the lake.

_____

2. The girl called her.

_____

3. The bird flew there.

_____

WRITE AWAY

Look around you. What is happening? On a sheet of paper, write three sentences that tell what you see. Use exact nouns.

Lively Verbs

Like nouns, verbs can add a lot of interest to your writing. It is important to choose the right verb to give a clear picture of what is happening.

Read this sentence.

The horses **ran** in the field.

Here is the same sentence written three different ways. Look at the lively verbs. They give more details.

The horses **galloped** in the field.

The horses **raced** in the field.

The horses **dashed** in the field.

If you choose lively verbs, the reader will enjoy your work. He or she will know exactly what you are saying, too.

Write each sentence using a lively verb.

1. Dan **made** a fruit salad.

_____

2. He **cut** some walnuts.

_____

WRITE AWAY

Look around you. What is happening? On a sheet of paper, write three sentences that tell what you see. Use lively verbs.

Add Adjectives

An **adjective** is a word that tells how something looks, feels, tastes, sounds, or smells. An adjective also tells how many. Adding adjectives to a sentence adds interest and also gives the reader a more exact picture of your idea.

Read this sentence.

The cows eat grass.

What picture do you get in your mind? How many cows are there? What is the grass like? Here is the same sentence after adding adjectives. Is this the same picture you thought about?

The **three black** cows eat **tall, sweet** grass.

As you can see, adjectives help you get the exact picture in your mind. Adjectives make an idea clear.

Look at the picture. Then write a sentence using each word. Use at least two adjectives in each sentence.

1. frozen yogurt _____

_____

2. dog _____

_____

WRITE AWAY

Think about a bee. Then, on a sheet of paper, write two sentences that describe it. See how many adjectives you can use.

The Reader's Senses

Think about a time when something strange happened. You may have written a letter telling someone about the event. What did you describe?

Writing with good details is a special skill. You want the reader to see, smell, taste, hear, and feel everything that you did. To be a good writer, you should choose words that have to do with the **reader's senses.**

Here are some sense words. They are all adjectives.

   Looks: red, round, shiny

   Smells: rotten, burnt, smoky

   Tastes: sweet, juicy, chocolate

   Sounds: loud, soft, crunchy

   Feels: smooth, rough, hot

Choose adjectives carefully. Make the reader feel that he or she is "there."

Look at each picture. Choose sense words to describe it.

1.

2.

Looks _____   Looks _____

Smells _____   Sounds _____

Tastes _____   Feels _____

36

Words That Paint a Picture

Words can help a reader see, feel, hear, taste, and touch. Words can paint a picture in the reader's mind. There is another way that you can paint a picture for a reader. You can write about two things that are alike. You **compare** them.

The **room** was as hot as **an oven.**

Here, the writer compares a room to an oven. You know how hot an oven can get. The room must be very hot, too!

Read each word picture. Underline the two things that are being compared. Then tell how they are alike.

1. José ran like the wind.

_____

2. Max's heart beat as loud as a drum.

_____

3. The building was as tall as a giant.

_____

WRITE AWAY

Finish the sentence below. Add words that help paint a picture.

The pillow _____.

Synonyms

You know that adjectives can add zip to any writing. Here is another way to make your writing more interesting. Choose a **synonym.**

A synonym is a word that has almost the same meaning as another word. Sometimes one synonym is better than another in a sentence.

Here is one sentence that uses different synonyms.

It was a **pretty** day for a picnic.

It was a **beautiful** day for a picnic.

It was a **lovely** day for a picnic.

Write a synonym for the underlined word in each sentence.

1. Raccoon climbed a <u>big</u> tree.   Synonym _____

2. He looked inside a <u>little</u> hole.   Synonym _____

3. He saw some <u>mad</u> bees.   Synonym _____

4. Raccoon <u>ran</u> away from the bees. Synonym _____

WRITE AWAY

Do you know what a **thesaurus** is? A thesaurus is a book that shows synonyms for many words. Choose one word from above. Ask a family member to help you look up the word in a thesaurus. Write the synonyms on a sheet of paper.

Antonyms

An **antonym** is a word that means the opposite of another word. Here are some antonyms.

walk—run   fast—slow   tall—short

Antonyms help readers paint a picture in their mind. The words show a reader how two things are different.

The **little** girl was eating a **big** slice of watermelon.

The **bright** sun showed through the **dark** clouds.

Read each sentence. Look at the underlined word. Write an antonym from the box to complete each sentence.

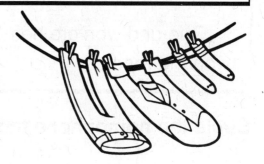

cold   dry   opened   clean

1. Erika washed the <u>dirty</u> clothes to make them _____.

2. She hung the <u>wet</u> clothes outside so they would _____.

3. Erika wanted to get out of the <u>hot</u> sun and into the

   _____ house.

4. She _____ the door and <u>shut</u> it when she got inside.

WRITE AWAY

On a sheet of paper, write a list of two antonym pairs that are not listed on this page. Then write sentences using the words.

Homophones

Spelling is an important part of writing. You want to spell all the words the right way. This will help your reader understand what you are saying.

Some words are tricky, though. These words are **homophones.** Homophones sound alike, but they have different spellings and meanings. Read these sentences. Which is correct?

Terrick **one** the race.

Terrick **won** the race.

<u>One</u> and <u>won</u> are homophones. The correct sentence is <u>Terrick won the race.</u>

Circle the homophone that correctly completes the sentence.

1. Tom went (to, too, two) the store.

2. He wanted to (by, buy) apples.

3. He liked the (red, read) apples best.

4. So, Tom bought (four, for) apples.

WRITE AWAY

On a sheet of paper, write three homophone pairs that are not listed on this page. Write sentences that use both words.

Joining Sentences with the Same Naming Part

Reading many short sentences can be boring. You can join some sentences so they will become more interesting. Look for sentences that have the same naming part. Then use the word <u>and</u> between the action parts.

The hamster ate food. **The hamster** drank water.

The hamster ate food <u>and</u> drank water.

Join each pair of sentences using the word <u>and</u>.
Write one sentence.

1. Hippo found a ball. Hippo got an umbrella.

   _____

2. He put them in the car. He drove to the beach.

   _____

3. The ocean water felt cool. The ocean water tasted salty.

   _____

WRITE AWAY

What else can Hippo do at the beach? On a sheet of paper, write sentences that tell more about Hippo. Look for sentences that you can join. Tell a friend or family member how you could join the short sentences.

Joining Sentences with the Same Action Part

You can join short sentences that have the same naming part. You can join short sentences that have the same action part, too. Use the word <u>and</u> between the naming parts. Then your writing will sound more interesting.

Pam **saw a mouse.** Eric **saw a mouse.**

Pam <u>and</u> Eric **saw a mouse.**

Join each pair of sentences using the word <u>and</u>. Write one sentence.

1. Jan worked in the garden. Alex worked in the garden.

_____

2. Fruits grew in it. Vegetables grew in it.

_____

3. A butterfly flew into their garden. A bee flew into their garden.

_____

_____

WRITE AWAY

What could happen in the garden? On a sheet of paper, write sentences that tell more about the garden. Look for sentences that you can join. Tell a friend or family member how you could join the short sentences.

Joining Sentences to List Words

Sometimes you might tell about three or more items. Each sentence has the same pattern. The naming part is the same, or the action part is the same. The sentences are very short. You can join these sentences in a list. You use the word <u>and</u>. You write a **comma (,)** between the words in the list.

Mary ate a **sandwich.** Mary ate a **pear.** Mary ate a **banana.**

Mary ate a **sandwich,** a **pear,** <u>and</u> a **banana.**

Fish are in the pond. **Frogs** are in the pond. **Turtles** are in the pond.

Fish, frogs, <u>and</u> **turtles** are in the pond.

Combine each set of sentences using the word <u>and</u>. Write one sentence.

1. Mr. West cooked fish. Mr. West cooked beans. Mr. West cooked peas.

_____

2. Jill bought milk. Kim bought milk. Ron bought milk.

_____

3. Mrs. Luna bought eggs. Mrs. Luna bought cheese. Mrs. Luna bought yogurt.

_____

43

Sentence Length

When you write, you want your sentences to sound like you are talking. You want them to flow. You can write short sentences and long sentences.

Read these sets of sentences.

Fox was hungry. Fox looked for food. Fox saw some grapes. The grapes were too high. Fox was not happy. Fox left.

Fox was hungry and looked for food. Fox saw some grapes. The grapes were too high. Fox was not happy and left.

Sentences that have different lengths make writing interesting.

Read the story. Rewrite it using sentences that have different lengths.

The lion got caught in a net. The lion roared for help. The mouse heard the roar. The mouse ran to help. The mouse chewed the net. The lion was free.

_____

_____

_____

_____

WRITE AWAY

Choose a nursery rhyme. On a sheet of paper, tell the rhyme in your own words. Remember to use long sentences and short sentences.

Sentence Beginnings

> Sometimes you might begin several sentences with the same noun. Do you think a reader would enjoy reading these sentences? A good writer changes the beginning of sentences. Sometimes the writer will use a pronoun in place of the noun. Remember that the pronouns are I, you, he, she, it, we, and they.
>
> **The ant** climbed up the picnic table. **The ant** got the watermelon.
>
> **The ant** climbed up the picnic table. **It** got the watermelon.

Read the story. Write it a different way. Write sentences that have different beginnings.

Hen liked to eat corn. Hen ate corn in the morning. Hen ate corn at night. Hen thought, "I am eating too much corn." So, Hen went for a jog.

_____

_____

_____

_____

WRITE AWAY

On a sheet of paper, add to the story about Hen. Tell what she does when she jogs. Try to use sentences with different beginnings.

Run-on Sentences

A **run-on sentence** is a sentence that is hard to understand. It has two naming parts and two action parts. An end mark is missing, too.

Here is a run-on sentence.   Kim is late she missed the bus.

You can fix a run-on sentence two ways.

- Join the two sentences. Add a comma **(,).** Write the word <u>and</u>, <u>or</u>, or <u>but</u>.   Kim is late, **and** she missed the bus.
- Write two sentences.   Kim is late. **She** missed the bus.

Correct each run-on sentence. Write the new sentence or sentences on the line.

1. Pat got out a paintbrush he got paints, too.

_____

2. He looked for paper Pat could not find it.

_____

3. Pat went to the store he bought paper.

_____

WRITE AWAY

Here is a very long run-on sentence. How would you fix it? On a sheet of paper, write the new sentences.

Leslie could not find her kitten she looked in the kitchen the living room and the bathroom Leslie finally found the kitten it was asleep under the bed.

Name _____ Date _____

Proofreading Sentences

You have learned a lot about sentences. You have practiced writing interesting sentences, too. Now it is time for you to practice proofreading them! When you proofread, you look for mistakes.

Look at the Proofreading Marks on page 114. You use these marks to show how to fix mistakes.

Here is an example of how to correct a sentence using proofreading marks.

Jack and jill went up a hill.

Correct each sentence. Use proofreading marks.

1. Greg went to the park on friday

2. he took kite.

3. Greg had fun fling kite

WRITE AWAY

Ask a friend or family member to write sentences on the lines below. Tell them to make three mistakes. Find the mistakes and correct them using the proofreading marks.

_____

_____

_____

_____

Self-Assessment: Sentences

You know a lot about writing sentences now. Are you ready to write? Use the writing process to help you. Follow the steps.

Prewriting

1. What is your favorite snack? List three.

   _____ _____ _____

2. Which do you like the most? Circle it.

3. List three details that tell why you like the snack.

   Detail 1 _____

   Detail 2 _____

   Detail 3 _____

4. Describe the snack. Use sense words.

   _____

   _____

   _____

   _____

Drafting

On a sheet of paper, write sentences about your favorite snack. Use your ideas from prewriting. Don't worry about making mistakes! Just get the sentences on paper.

Self-Assessment: Sentences, part 2

Revising

Look at the sentences in your draft. How can you make them better? Use the revising hints on page 14 to revise your sentences. Then write a clean copy of your sentences below.

_____

_____

_____

_____

_____

Proofreading

You need to proofread your sentences. Read your work three times. Look for a different mistake each time. You can use the Proofreading Checklist on page 113 to help you. Don't forget to use the Proofreading Marks on page 114.

Publishing

Now it is time to make a clean copy of your sentences. You can handwrite them on a sheet of paper. Or, you can type them on the computer. Don't forget to add a title and a picture. Now you can share your sentences!

Congratulations! You wrote great sentences. As you can see, the writing process is easy and fun!

What Is a Paragraph?

You know how to write great sentences. Now you will put sentences together to make a **paragraph.** A paragraph is a group of sentences that tell about one main idea. The **main idea** is what the paragraph is mostly about. The first sentence usually tells the main idea. The other sentences tell more about the main idea.

The first line of each paragraph is **indented.** This means that the first word is moved one finger space to the right. Here is a paragraph.

A frog has strong, long back legs. The legs help it jump on land. The legs help it swim in water. The legs help a frog stay safe. The frog uses its legs to get away from animals that will eat it.

Write the main idea of the paragraph above.

_____

Write two sentences that tell more about the main idea.

Sentence 1 _____

Sentence 2 _____

WRITE AWAY

On a sheet of paper, write a paragraph. Use the sentence below as the first sentence. It is your main idea. Write other sentences that tell more about the main idea. Don't forget to indent!

A computer helps people.

50

Parts of a Paragraph

A **paragraph** is a group of sentences that tell about one main idea. A paragraph has three parts.

- The **topic sentence** is often the first sentence. It tells the main idea.

- **Detail sentences** tell more about the main idea. They give details.

- The **ending sentence** is the last sentence. It is like the topic sentence, but it uses different words.

Read the paragraph below. Then follow the directions.

Rita bought a ball for her cat. The ball is blue. It has a bell inside. Rita rolls the ball on the floor. Her cat chases it. Rita's cat likes to play with the ball.

1. Underline the main idea sentence.

2. Number the detail sentences.

3. Circle the ending sentence.

WRITE AWAY

Is the paragraph above a good paragraph? Why or why not? Tell why you think as you do.

_____

_____

_____

51

Paragraph Order

When you write, you follow the steps in the writing process. You follow a special writing order. The sentences in a paragraph have a certain order, too.

- The first sentence is often the **topic sentence.** It tells the main idea of the paragraph.

- The middle sentences are the **detail sentences.** They form the body of the paragraph. They give details about the topic.

- The last sentence is the **ending sentence.** It tells about the main idea again, but it uses different words.

Write _1_ through _5_ to show the best order of the sentences in the paragraph.

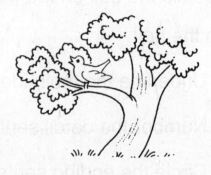

_____ It sang a pretty song.

_____ I looked out the window.

_____ I was very glad that I woke up early!

_____ I woke up early on Saturday.

_____ I saw a redbird.

WRITE AWAY

Look out a window. What do you see? On a sheet of paper, write a paragraph. Follow the correct paragraph order. Underline your topic sentence. Circle your ending sentence.

The Right Size Paragraph

Every paragraph has a **topic.** The topic is what you are writing about. Some topics can be very big. Other topics are too small. You must choose one main idea in the topic. The main idea needs to be the right size. You should be able to clearly explain the main idea in three or four details.

Suppose that you want to write about horses. That is a large topic! You could write about how they grow or the jobs they do. You could even write about different kinds of horses.

Topic: horses
Main idea: jobs horses do
Detail 1: police horses
Detail 2: horses pull things
Detail 3: people ride horses for fun

Look at the topics below. Then choose a main idea for each topic. Write three details about the main idea.

1. Topic: birds

Main idea: _____

Detail 1: _____

Detail 2: _____

Detail 3: _____

2. Topic: seasons

Main idea: _____

Detail 1: _____

Detail 2: _____

Detail 3: _____

WRITE AWAY

On a sheet of paper, write a paragraph using one of your main ideas. Write sentences that are in the correct order.

Drawing a Picture

Sometimes you are given a topic to write about. You know that you need to choose a main idea that is the right size. The main idea needs to have three or four details. How do you find the details to write about? You can draw a picture!

A picture will help you remember to include the details about people, places, and other things that are important to the main idea. Remember that details will help the reader understand everything you are saying.

Look at the topic. Then choose a main idea. Draw a picture about the main idea. Next, write three details that you see in your picture.

Topic: farm

Main idea: _____

Detail 1: _____

Detail 2: _____

Detail 3: _____

WRITE AWAY

On a sheet of paper, write a paragraph using the main idea above. Remember to write sentences that help your reader understand your main idea.

Listing What You Need to Know

> Sometimes you are given a topic to write about that you don't know much about. You might know some details, but you think there is more information that you should include in your paragraph.
>
> Before you begin to write, make a list of what you know about the topic. Look at the list to decide if you are missing important information. Then look for the missing details. You can ask someone to help you.

Look at the topic. Then choose a main idea. List what you know. Are you missing some information? Write what you need to know.

Topic: whales

Main idea: _____

Detail 1: _____

Detail 2: _____

Detail 3: _____

What I need to know: _____

What I need to know: _____

WRITE AWAY

Look at the information that you need to know. Where could you find the information? Write your ideas on a sheet of paper. You might ask a friend or family member to give you some more ideas.

Writing a Topic Sentence

Remember that a paragraph tells about one main idea of a topic. A **topic sentence** is the sentence that tells the main idea. The topic sentence is usually the first sentence in a paragraph. You want the topic sentence to catch a reader's interest. Then the reader will want to keep reading.

Read these sentences. Which sentence is more interesting?

Birds make nests.

Birds build a special home called a nest.

Both sentences talk about the same main idea—making a nest. But the second sentence uses words to make the main idea more interesting.

Read each topic sentence. Rewrite the sentence to make it more interesting.

1. Water is important.

_____

2. Apples are good to eat.

_____

3. Monkeys live in the jungle.

_____

WRITE AWAY

Choose one of the topic sentences you wrote above. On a sheet of paper, write a paragraph using the topic sentence.

Writing Detail Sentences

Detail sentences make up the body of the paragraph. They give facts or examples about the main idea. They help the reader understand the topic. They also keep the reader interested. Here are some hints to help you write detail sentences.

- Choose the most interesting details.
- Choose details that give clear examples.
- Write three or four details.

Read the detail sentences about bird nests. Notice how they tell more about the main idea.

Birds build a special home called a nest. **Most nests are made with twigs and grass. Some birds use mud to hold the pieces together. Other birds put string or cloth in the nest to make it soft.**

**Read the topic sentence. Follow the directions.
Use a sheet of paper.**

Topic: spring

Main idea: things begin to grow

Topic sentence: Spring is a time when things begin to grow.

1. Write three details. Tell what begins to grow in spring.

2. Circle the best detail. Write a detail sentence.

Writing an Ending Sentence

An **ending sentence** is the last sentence in a paragraph. It tells about the main idea again. It uses different words from the topic sentence.

Read the paragraph about bird nests. Look carefully at the topic sentence and the ending sentence.

Birds build a special home called a nest. Most nests are made with twigs and grass. Some birds use mud to hold the pieces together. Other birds put string or cloth in the nest to make it soft. **The birds work hard to build the perfect place to live.**

Read the paragraph below. Then write an ending sentence.

Danny loved to read. He read books about animals. He read books about plants. His favorite books told stories about silly people.

_____

_____

WRITE AWAY

Sometimes it is a good idea to write several ending sentences. Then you can choose the one that sounds best. Write another ending sentence to the story above. Ask a friend or family member to tell which ending he or she likes best.

_____

_____

58

Starting to Write

Suppose that you have finished prewriting for a topic. You know your main idea. You know which details you will use. Now it is time to start your draft. You get a sheet of paper. However, you are not sure what to write. What can you do?

It might be helpful to begin writing the part that you know best. Once there is something on your paper, the rest of the words will come more easily.

Here are the prewriting ideas for a topic. What should you write first? Follow the directions.

Topic: camping

Main idea: fun things to do

Detail 1: sleep in a tent

Detail 2: take hikes

Detail 3: see wild animals

Detail 4: sit by a campfire

1. Circle the detail you know the most about.

2. Write a sentence on a sheet of paper about the detail you circled.

WRITE AWAY

On a sheet of paper, write a paragraph using the information above. Remember to write all the parts of a paragraph.

Keeping to the Topic

A **paragraph** is a group of sentences that tell about one main idea. All the details in the paragraph must tell about the topic. You should take out sentences that do not tell about the topic.

Read the paragraph. Find the sentence that does not belong.

> Sam and Pam pulled weeds in the garden.
> Suddenly, a snake wiggled by. Sam jumped back.
> The tomatoes were huge! Pam laughed. "It is only a
> little garden snake," she said.

The sentence that does not belong is <u>The tomatoes were huge!</u>
The story is about a garden snake, not tomatoes.

**Order the sentences to make a paragraph. Write <u>1</u> through <u>5</u>.
The topic sentence has been done for you. Put an <u>X</u> in front of
the sentence you do not need.**

__1__ <u>Fred wanted to learn how to play a guitar.</u>

_____ After one year, Fred knew how to play a guitar.

_____ Fred would also cook.

_____ He took lessons for many months.

_____ Fred practiced many hours, too.

_____ So he bought a guitar.

WRITE AWAY

On a sheet of paper, write the paragraph above.

Paragraphs That Flow

The paragraphs you write should sound like you are talking. The paragraphs should flow from one sentence to another. Some words help the sentences in a paragraph flow. These words are also, because, and too. Read this paragraph.

My family and I are going to the park. Mark wants to come, **too.**

We think Jen will **also** come. We will all have fun.

Look at the word too. It is at the end of a sentence. Place a comma **(,)** behind the word in front of too.

Read the paragraph. Add the words too and also. Use the Proofreading Marks on page 114 to show where to put the words.

Jason was playing with his little red robot. He made the robot go left. He made the robot go right. Jason made it roll under the chair. He laughed when his cat flew out from under the chair. The cat did not like playing with the little red robot.

WRITE AWAY

Suppose there is a special show on television. It comes on after you go to bed. Why should you get to stay up? On a sheet of paper, write a paragraph telling three reasons. Use the words too, because, and also in your paragraph.

Time-Order Words

Think about a time you told a story. You told the events in order. You told what happened at the beginning. Then, you told what happened in the middle. Finally, you told how it ended.

You might have used **time-order words.** The words helped you tell when something happened. Here are some time-order words.

before	after	first	next	then
during	later	soon	now	finally

Time-order words help tell story events, too.

Leo got ready for bed. **First,** he washed his face. **Then,** he brushed his teeth. **Next,** he put on his pajamas. **Finally,** Leo was ready for bed.

Read the paragraph. Write time-order words to tell the order things happen.

Making a peanut butter sandwich is easy.

_____, you spread peanut butter on one

slice of bread. _____, you spread jelly on top of the peanut

butter. _____, you place another slice of bread on the jelly.

Yum! _____, you can eat the peanut butter and jelly sandwich.

WRITE AWAY

On a sheet of paper, write a paragraph telling how to make another type of sandwich. Use time-order words.

Writing Pattern: Main Idea and Details

Think about a time you made a craft. You put a pattern on paper. Then you traced around the pattern. When you cut out the shape, it was the same size and shape as the pattern. Your craft was going to look just like the one in the pattern.

Writers follow a pattern, too. They follow a **writing pattern.** The pattern helps them arrange a paragraph. They order the information a special way.

One kind of writing pattern is called **main idea and details.** In this kind of pattern, you write about one main idea. You add details that tell more about the main idea. A web can help you plan this kind of paragraph.

Look at your shirt. Tell about it. Use the Main Idea and Details Web on page 119. It will help you make a plan. Then follow the directions below to complete the web.

1. What is the main idea that you will write about? Write it in the center oval.

2. What details should you write? Think about details that will help a reader understand what your shirt looks like. Write one detail in each circle of the web.

WRITE AWAY

On a sheet of paper, write a paragraph that tells what your shirt looks like. Follow the steps in the writing process. They are listed on page 110.

Writing Pattern: Sequence of Events

Sometimes you will need to tell how to do something. You might also need to tell a story. To do this, you will have to tell the order that events happen. You will tell a **sequence.** You will be using a **sequence writing pattern** to tell the order.

A sequence chart can help you plan your writing. It helps you think about each step. You can plan which time-order words to use. Some time-order words are first, next, then, and finally.

Tell how to plant a seed. Use the Sequence Chart on page 120 to write the steps in order. Follow the directions below to complete the chart.

1. What step do you do first? Write it in the top box.

2. What step do you do last? Write it in the bottom box.

3. What steps do you do in between? Write time-order words on the lines. Then write the steps. Draw more boxes if you need to.

WRITE AWAY

On a sheet of paper, write a paragraph that tells how to plant a seed. Follow the steps in the writing process. They are listed on page 110.

Writing Pattern: Compare and Contrast

Sometimes you might write a paragraph to tell how two animals are alike. You will **compare** them. Then you will tell how they are different. You will **contrast** the animals. You will use a **compare and contrast writing pattern** in the paragraph.

A Venn diagram can help you plan what you will write. The diagram helps you think about the special parts of each item.

Compare and contrast a dog and cat. Use the Venn Diagram on page 121. Tell how they are alike. Tell how they are different. Follow the directions below to complete the diagram.

1. Label each circle. Write <u>dog</u> above one circle. Write <u>cat</u> above the other circle.

2. Look where the circles join. Write words that tell how a dog and cat are alike in this space.

3. In the circle under <u>dog</u>, write details about the dog. The details should tell how the dog is different from the cat.

4. In the circle under <u>cat</u>, write details about the cat. The details should tell how the cat is different from the dog.

WRITE AWAY

On a sheet of paper, write a paragraph about a chair and a table. Compare and contrast them. Follow the steps in the writing process listed on page 110.

Writing Pattern: Problem and Solution

A **problem** is something that is wrong. It needs to be fixed. A **solution** is the way to fix the problem. A **problem and solution writing pattern** is often useful if you are explaining something that is a problem.

When using this pattern, give clear examples and use exact details. You should also tell why the solution works. When you choose this pattern, a Problem and Solution Chart can help you plan your work.

Think about a problem that you had with a brother, sister, or other family member. Use the Problem and Solution Chart on page 122 to explain the details. Follow the directions below to complete the chart.

I. Write the problem. List two or three details about the problem.

2. Write the solution. Tell why the solution worked.

WRITE AWAY

On a sheet of paper, write a paragraph that tells about the problem you had with a family member. Explain the solution. Follow the steps in the writing process.

66

Writing Pattern: Cause and Effect

What happens when you fall down? You might cry. The first action makes the second action happen.

The first action is the **cause.** A cause is why something has happened. An **effect** is what happened. Falling down is the cause. Crying is the effect.

The **cause and effect writing pattern** is useful if you are telling about events. You should clearly state the cause and the effect. The reader must understand how the two events go together. You can use a Cause and Effect Chart to help you plan your writing.

Think about a time you got hurt. Use the Cause and Effect Charts on page 123 to explain the details. Follow the directions below to complete the charts.

1. Write the cause. Use exact nouns and verbs to explain the details.

2. Write the effect, or what happened. Use sense words so that the audience can "see" the effect.

WRITE AWAY

On a sheet of paper, write a paragraph that tells about the time you got hurt. Clearly explain the cause and the effect. Follow the steps in the writing process.

67

Writing Pattern: Summary

Think about your last birthday. If someone asked you about it, what would you say? Would you describe the clothes you wore? Would you list every present that you got? Probably not, because you wouldn't want the person to get bored. You would tell only the most important details.

When you tell the most important details of an event, you are giving a **summary.** You tell who, what, where, when, why, and how. You might use the **summary writing pattern** to give your audience a short description without telling the whole story. You can use a Summary Chart to help you plan your writing.

Think again about your last birthday. Use the Summary Chart on page 124. Follow the directions below to complete the chart.

1. Look at the left side of the box. Tell who, what, where, when, why, and how.

2. Use the details from the left side of the chart to tell about the party. Write only two or three sentences on the right side.

WRITE AWAY

On a sheet of paper, write a paragraph that summarizes your birthday. Add a few more details that you think your audience might like to hear. Follow the steps in the writing process.

Adding Details

Once you have revised your draft, it is a good idea to set it aside for a little while. You have worked on it for a long time. It may be hard to see your mistakes.

Look at your writing again later. Read it out loud. Listen for special kinds of problems.

- Listen for details and ideas that a reader might not understand.
- Listen for details and ideas that a reader would want to know more about.

Then revise your paragraph. Add more details. Make the paragraph easier to read and understand.

Read the paragraph out loud. Then answer the questions and follow the directions. Use a sheet of paper.

Cecil loved his job. He liked to hold a ball. He liked to dance with the clowns. Everyone clapped for Cecil.

1. What is hard to understand in the paragraph?

2. What would you like to know more about?

3. Rewrite the paragraph above so it has more details to help a reader understand the story.

Choosing a Title

The **title** is the name of a piece of writing. You want to have an exciting title. An exciting title will make the reader want to read on.

Read these story titles. Which story would you like to read?

The Green Turtle

Tim Turtle Takes a Trip

Most likely, you would like to read the second story. The title sounds like it would be more fun!

Here are some hints for choosing an exciting title.

- Think about the main idea.
- Look for words that are repeated in your writing.
- Choose words that match the writing. (A silly story should have a silly title. A report should have a serious title.)
- Important words begin with a capital letter. The words a, an, the, for, at, and in do not begin with a capital letter except when they are the first word in the title.

Read the titles of the nursery rhymes below.
Rewrite each one to make a more interesting title.

I. Little Bo Peep _____

2. Little Miss Muffet _____

WRITE AWAY

What is the title of your favorite book? On a sheet of paper, tell if it is a good title or not. Tell why or why not.

Self-Assessment: Paragraphs

You know how to write great paragraphs now. It's time to use these skills in the writing process. Just follow these steps.

Follow the directions. Use a sheet of paper.

Prewriting

1. What do you know a lot about? List three topics.

2. Which of your topics do you think is the most interesting? Circle it.

3. Write your main idea.

4. List three details that tell about your main idea.

5. Who would like to know about this idea? Write who your audience is.

6. What writing pattern will best help your audience understand the topic? Circle it.

   Main idea and details   Sequence of events   Compare and contrast
   Problem and solution   Cause and effect   Summary

7. Write your topic sentence. Remember that it should tell about your main idea. It should catch a reader's interest.

71

Self-Assessment: Paragraphs, part 2

Drafting

On a sheet of paper, write your topic sentence. Write at least three detail sentences. Then write an ending sentence. Don't worry about making mistakes! Just get the sentences on paper.

Revising

Read your paragraph. Ask yourself these questions.

- Does it make sense?

- Where can I add exact or lively words?

- Are the sentences long and short?

- Do the sentences begin with different kinds of words?

- Did I use words that my audience can understand?

Write your paragraph again. Make the changes.

Proofreading

Read your paragraph three times. Look for mistakes.

- Look for mistakes with capital letters.

- Look for mistakes with end marks and commas.

- Look for spelling mistakes.

You can use the Proofreading Checklist on page 113 as a guide. Use the Proofreading Marks on page 114 to show where the mistakes are.

Publishing

Make a clean copy of your paragraph. You can handwrite it on a sheet of paper or type it on the computer. Don't forget to add a title! You might even want to draw a picture to go along with your paragraph. Then share it with your audience!

Personal Story

A **personal story** is a fun story to write. It tells about something that has happened to the writer. When you write a personal story, you are writing about YOU!

Here are some hints to help you write a personal story.

- Tell about one event that has happened to you.
- Use the pronouns I, me, and my.
- Tell how you feel in one part of the story.
- Tell the events in order.

Here is an example of a personal story.

I took my dog Spot for a walk yesterday. Spot walked nicely on his leash at first. Then, Spot saw a squirrel. He raced after the squirrel and pulled me. I fell down. Finally, I told Spot to behave. He was nice for the rest of the walk.

Follow the directions below.

1. Think about some things that have happened to you. Write a list of three ideas.

   _____

   _____

   _____

2. Which idea would make an exciting personal story? Circle it.

Personal Story, part 2

Use the Prewriting Survey on pages 111–112. Plan your personal story. Then answer the questions below. They will help you plan more details.

1. What happened at the beginning of the story?

_____

2. What topic sentence could you write to catch a reader's interest?

_____

3. What happened in the middle of the story?

_____

4. What are some vivid verbs that describe the events?

_____

5. How did you feel? Write at least three words.

_____

6. What happened at the end of the story?

_____

_____

WRITE AWAY

You have been prewriting a personal story. Now it's time to start your draft on a sheet of paper. Review the hints on page 73. Then follow the rest of the steps in the writing process to finish your story.

Person Description

Everybody is special! A **person description** tells how someone is special. It also tells why someone is special. You will need to choose words to help readers "see" the person in their minds.

Here are some hints to help you write a person description.

- Tell what someone is like.
- Choose sense words that help readers see, smell, feel, and hear the person.
- Choose lively and interesting adjectives.

Here is an example of a person description.

    The clown looked very cheerful. His nose was painted red like a giant tomato. His mouth turned up in a huge grin. He wore a big yellow bow. Bright circles covered the clown's pants and shirt. His big blue shoes slapped the ground as he walked.

Follow the directions below.

1. Choose a person you think is interesting or special. Write the name.

_____

2. On a sheet of paper, draw a picture of this person. Add details that show how this person is special.

Person Description, part 2

Use the Prewriting Survey on pages 111–112. Plan your person description. Then answer the questions below on a sheet of paper. They will help you paint a clear picture of the person.

1. What is special about the person? Explain.

2. What are some face or body parts that stand out?

3. Can you paint a picture of the person? Can you compare something on the person to another object? (Hint: The clown's nose was compared to a tomato.)

4. Look at the picture you drew. What lively adjectives can you use?

5. Think about a topic sentence. What could you say about the person that would catch a reader's interest?

WRITE AWAY

You have been prewriting ideas for a person description. You will write your draft now on a sheet of paper. Review the hints on page 75. Then follow the rest of the steps in the writing process.

Name _____ Date _____

Place Description

A **place description** tells about a place. The writer uses words to help readers "feel" they are right there. The readers should see, hear, taste, smell, and feel everything with the writer.

Here are some hints to help you write a place description.

- Choose sense words that help readers see, smell, taste, feel, and hear the place.
- Choose a way to lead the person through the place. (Describe a place from top to bottom. Or describe a place from left to right.)

Here is an example of a place description.

Max looked at the clear blue water. He could see the sunlight dance on its surface. Children splashed and squealed as they tossed a ball to each other. In the distance, Max could see a red sailboat glide across the lake. Its white sail spread out to catch the gusty wind.

Use the Prewriting Survey on pages III–II2. Plan your place description. Use the hints above to help you. Name the place that you will write about below. Then, on a sheet of paper, write a draft that tells about it.

Place _____

77

Place Description, part 2

Look at your draft. Then answer the questions below.
They will help you revise your place description.

1. How did you lead the reader through the place? Did you describe
   the place from bottom to top, right to left, or some other way?

   _____

2. What feeling did you want to share with the reader? What words did
   you use to help the reader feel this way?

   Feeling _____

   Words _____

3. Name the senses that you use in your writing.

   _____

4. Does your paragraph make sense? Why or why not? _____

   _____

5. Which lively or exact word in your paragraph do you think is the
   best? Why?

   _____

WRITE AWAY

Revise your place description. Use the ideas above to make it better.
Then follow the rest of the steps in the writing process.

Name _____ Date _____

Thing Description

A description paints a picture with words. So a **thing description** tells about a thing. When you choose a thing to describe, you need to give enough details to let the reader picture what you are describing.

Here are some hints to help you write a thing description.

- Choose a thing that is interesting.

- Choose a thing that can be described in about three sentences.

- Describe the parts that the audience will want to know more about.

- Choose words that help readers see, smell, taste, feel, and hear the thing.

Here is an example of a descriptive paragraph about a thing.

The cute little house next door sits on top of the hill. Its yellow walls and green trim shine in the sun. A white fence surrounds the beautiful front yard. The lush green grass spreads like a carpet all around it. Bright flowers wave gently in the breeze. The house looks like it should be in a storybook.

Choose a thing to write about. Use the Prewriting Survey on pages 111–112. Plan your thing description and use the hints above to help you. Write a draft of your description on a sheet of paper.

Thing Description, part 2

Look at your draft. Use the questions below to revise your thing description.

1. Will your reader be interested in this thing? Why or why not?

_____

2. Name the senses that you use in your writing. Which words go along with these senses?

_____

3. Do the details clearly tell about the thing? How do you know?

_____

4. Did you use any of these verbs: <u>is</u>, <u>are</u>, <u>was</u>, <u>were</u>, <u>am</u>, or <u>be</u>? If so, which lively verbs could you write in their place?

_____

5. You can compare two things that are not alike to help a reader understand something. What can you compare the thing to?

_____

WRITE AWAY

Use the questions above to help you revise your thing description. Then follow the rest of the steps in the writing process.

Name _____ Date _____

How-to Paragraph

A **how-to paragraph** tells the steps needed to do a task. It is important to tell each step in the correct order.

Here are some hints to help you write a how-to paragraph.

- The topic sentence tells what you will teach.

- Include a detail sentence that tells the materials needed.

- Give the steps in order.

- Use time-order words to make the steps clear.

- Write a title that names the task.

Here is an example of a how-to paragraph.

How to Make a Diorama

A diorama is a scene in a box. To make a rain forest diorama, you will need a shoebox, pictures, craft supplies, glue, markers, and scissors. First, color the inside of the box so that the sides look like a rain forest. Then, cut out pictures of rain forest animals. Finally, glue the pictures in the box. Now you can tell your friends about the rain forest.

Follow the directions below.

1. Think about some things that you know how to do well. Write two ideas.

_____

_____

2. Which idea do you think a reader would like to learn about? Circle it.

How-to Paragraph, part 2

**Use the Prewriting Survey on pages 111–112 to plan your
how-to paragraph. Then answer the questions below.
They will help make your how-to paragraph clear.**

1. What do you want to teach others to do? _____

2. What materials do you need? _____

   _____

3. In your mind, play a movie of yourself doing the task. List each step
   on the Sequence Chart. It is on page 120.

4. Will a reader understand each step? If not, how can you make

   a step clearer? _____

   _____

5. Which time-order words can you use? _____

6. Who is your audience? _____

7. What words will your audience understand? _____

   _____

WRITE AWAY

You have been prewriting your how-to paragraph. Now it's time to start
your draft on a sheet of paper. Review the hints on page 81. Then follow
the steps in the writing process. Don't forget a title!

Information Paragraph

Some paragraphs tell about one topic, or main idea. This kind of paragraph is an **information paragraph.** It includes two or three details about the topic. The details are facts, or pieces of information that are true.

Here are some hints to help you write an information paragraph.

- Choose one main idea.

- Write an introduction about the idea.

- Write important facts that tell about the main idea.

- Do not include how you feel about the topic.

- Write an ending sentence. Tell the main idea again in a new way.

- Write a title that tells the main idea.

Here is an example of an information paragraph.

A Canoe

A long time ago, some Native Americans made canoes out of trees. They chopped the trees down and cut them in half. Then, they used fire to burn away the inside. Where there was a dip in the middle, the people filled it with hot water to make the wood soft. They finished carving out the wood. After much work, the canoe was ready. They had turned a tree into a canoe!

What topic do you know about? Use the Prewriting Survey on pages 111–112 to plan an information paragraph. Then look at the hints above. They will help you write a draft on a sheet of paper. Next, revise and proofread your draft. The next page will help you publish your paragraph.

Information Paragraph, part 2

You have followed four steps in the writing process. Now it is time to publish your information paragraph. Answer the questions below. They will help you do your best work.

I. Read the paragraph. Which words are important? Write three.

_____

2. How can you use these words to make a title? Write several

title ideas. _____

_____

3. How will you show your work? (notebook paper, computer printout,

booklet, etc.) _____

4. Should you add a picture to make an idea or a detail clear? Why or

why not? _____

5. Where is the best place to add a picture, map, diagram, time line, or

chart? Why? _____

WRITE AWAY

Publish your information paragraph. Use the answers above to help you. You may want to publish your information paragraph on the computer. Review the steps on page 16 to get ideas.

Compare and Contrast Paragraph

When you show how two things are alike, you **compare** them. When you show how two things are different, you **contrast** them. In a **compare and contrast paragraph,** you show how two people, places, or things are alike and different.

Here are some hints that will help you write a compare and contrast paragraph.

- Write a topic sentence that names the two people, places, or things.
- Tell how the two are alike. Use exact examples.
- Tell how the two are different. Use exact examples.

Here is an example of a compare and contrast paragraph.

A cardinal and blue jay sat at the feeder. The cardinal was bright red. It had a crest on its head. The blue jay was much bigger than the cardinal. Its feathers were blue. It had a black bill. Both birds loved the seeds, though. They ate them all up.

Choose two foods. Use the Prewriting Survey on pages 111–112. Plan a compare and contrast paragraph about the foods. Then write a draft on a sheet of paper and revise it.

85

Compare and Contrast Paragraph, part 2

You have followed three steps in the writing process. Now it is time to proofread your paragraph. Answer the questions below. They will help you proofread your work.

1. How many sentences are in your paragraph? _____

   Do they all begin with a capital letter? _____

2. How many questions did you write? _____

   Do they end with a question mark? _____

3. Do all other sentences have the correct end mark? How do

   you know? _____

   _____

4. Did you write a list of three or more things? If so, did you use a

   comma to separate those items in the list? _____

5. Homophones are words that sound the same but have different spellings and meanings. <u>To</u>, <u>too</u>, and <u>two</u> are homophones. Which homophones did you use in your writing?

   _____

6. Which words might be spelled wrong? Look them up in a dictionary.

WRITE AWAY

Use the questions above to help you proofread your paragraph. Then publish it. Share the paragraph with a friend or family member.

Rhyme

Rhyming words are words that end with the same sound. <u>Car</u> and <u>star</u> are rhyming words. A **rhyme** is two or more lines that end with rhyming words. Many rhymes are silly or funny.

Here are some hints to help you write a rhyme.

- Write at least two lines.
- The lines should have a beat, or rhythm.
- End each line with a rhyming word.

Here is a rhyme.

Some pigs like mud to keep them **cool.**

But I prefer a swimming **pool.**

Follow the directions below.

1. Which animal would make a fun rhyme? Circle it.

   cat   bee   cow   pig   goat   hen

2. What words rhyme with the animal's name? Write as many words as you can.

   _____

   _____

   _____

Rhyme, part 2

Answer the questions to help you plan your rhyme.

1. Look at your list of words. What can your animal do with some of the words? List three ideas. You can be silly!

   Idea 1 _____

   Idea 2 _____

   Idea 3 _____

2. Get three sheets of drawing paper. Draw a picture of each idea you listed above.

3. Look at your pictures. Which do you think is the funniest? Put the other pictures away.

4. Are there more details that you can add to your picture? Draw the details now.

5. Write some sentences about your picture. They do not need to rhyme.

_____

_____

WRITE AWAY

Now it's time to write a rhyme. Use your ideas and your picture. Look at the hints on page 87. Write two lines of rhyme. Follow the writing process. Publish your rhyme. You might even like to write the rhyme on the picture you drew.

Poem

Writing a **poem** can be fun! It gives you a chance to tell how you feel. You can paint a picture with the words you write. While most poems rhyme, they do not have to.

Here are some hints to help you write a poem.

- Choose a topic that you feel strongly about.
- Choose colorful words that paint a picture.
- Use rhyming words if you want.
- Write a title that grabs the reader's attention.

Here are two poems that have the same topic. One rhymes, and one does not.

The Bee and the Frog
A tiny green frog
Was lying on a log
When he heard a buzzing bee.
He stuck out his tongue.
And then he got stung.
He cried, "That really hurt me!"

The Bee and the Frog
The frog sat quietly.
It looked like it was sleeping.
But at the sound of a buzz,
Its large eyes snapped open.
A long tongue quickly flew out.
And then it went right back inside.
Buzz! Buzz! The bee flew away.

Tell what your favorite season is and why.

_____

_____

On a sheet of paper, draw a picture that goes along with the sentence you wrote above.

Poem, part 2

Use the Prewriting Survey on pages III–II2 to plan your poem. Then answer the questions below.

1. What are some things that you see in your favorite season?

   Write at least four words. _____

2. Choose one word above. Compare it to something else that is very different. Tell how they are alike using word pictures.

   _____

3. What do you feel during this season? Write four adjectives.

   _____

4. Choose one of the words above. Brainstorm a list of rhyming words for this word. Try to name at least five words.

   _____

5. Think of some sounds you might hear during this time of year. What words tell about these sounds? For example, the wind might <u>swoosh</u>.

   _____

WRITE AWAY

You have been prewriting ideas for a poem. Review the hints on page 89. They will help you paint a word picture. Then follow the rest of the steps in the writing process. Try to write a poem that is at least four lines long. The poem doesn't have to rhyme.

Name _____   Date _____

Friendly Letter

A **friendly letter** is a letter that you send to someone you know. It has five parts. They are the **heading, greeting, body, closing,** and **signature.** Find each part below.

heading — May 5, 2014

greeting — Dear Grandma,

body — Mom and I went on a picnic. We took sandwiches, apples, and lemonade. We had lots of fun. Mom says we can go on another picnic when you come to visit.

closing — Love,

signature — Shondra

Here are some hints that will help you write a friendly letter.

- Choose a person you know to write to.
- Write details that the reader will want to know.
- Be sure that your letter has five parts.
- Use capital letters and commas correctly.

Who could you write a friendly letter to? Write the name below. Use the Prewriting Survey on pages 111–112 to plan the letter. Then look at the hints above. Write a draft of a letter on a sheet of paper and revise it.

I will write a friendly letter to _____.

Friendly Letter, part 2

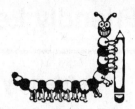

You have followed three steps in the writing process. Now it is time to proofread your letter. Answer the questions below on a sheet of paper. They will help you proofread your letter.

1. What date did you write in the letter? Did you begin the month with a capital letter?

2. What mark did you write between the date and the year?

3. What name did you write in the greeting? Does each word begin with a capital letter?

4. What mark did you write at the end of the greeting?

5. How many sentences did you write? Do they all begin with capital letters? Do they all have end marks?

6. What mark did you write at the end of the closing?

7. Which words might be spelled wrong? Circle them. Look them up in a dictionary.

WRITE AWAY

Publish your letter. Then send the letter to the person in the greeting.

Invitation

An **invitation** is another kind of letter. It asks someone to come somewhere. You might invite a friend to a birthday party. You might invite your aunt and uncle to watch you act in a play.

Here are some hints to help you write an invitation.

- Tell who is invited.
- Tell what the invitation is for.
- Tell where the event takes place.
- Tell when to come and leave.
- Use the five parts of a friendly letter.

Here is an invitation.

heading ─ October 28, 2013

greeting ─ Dear John,

body ─ Would you please come to my dance show? It is on Saturday. I will be dancing at North Fork School. The show begins at three o'clock and ends at five o'clock. I hope you can come!

closing ─ Your friend,

signature ─ Marta

Imagine that you are having a birthday party. Who could you invite? Write the name below. Use the Prewriting Survey on pages 111–112 to plan the invitation. Then look at the hints above. Write a draft of an invitation on a sheet of paper

I will invite _____ to my party.

Invitation, part 2

You have followed two steps in the writing process. Now it is time to revise your invitation. Answer the questions below on a sheet of paper. They will help you write an invitation that makes sense.

1. Does your reader know all the details for the party?
   Write the details that tell what, where, and when.

2. Are the details easy to understand? Why or why not?

3. What exact words did you use?

4. Can you join two sentences together? If so,
   write the new sentence.

5. How many long sentences do you have? How many short sentences
   do you have?

WRITE AWAY

Make a clean copy of your invitation. Use the ideas above to revise it.
Then follow the rest of the steps in the writing process to publish
your invitation.

Observation Log

An **observation log** is often used in science experiments. It tells what you did, what you saw, and what happened. An observation log often tells how something changes.

Here are some hints to help you write an observation log.

- Write the place where the events happen.
- Write the date and time.
- Use all five senses to describe what you see.
- Use exact words.
- Draw pictures. Name the parts of the pictures.

Here is an observation log.

Classroom Science Center
March 3, 2014 at 8:32 a.m.

At first, I thought the mealworms looked the same today as they did yesterday. But when I looked closer, I saw they were not moving very much. I held one in my hand. It had a soft tan color. I saw a piece of skin that I think came from it.

Look at the picture below. It shows a flower that is growing. Imagine that you are writing an observation log. Use the words to label the picture.

| roots |
| flower |
| stem |
| leaves |

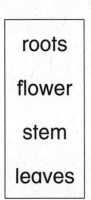

Observation Log, part 2

Use the Prewriting Survey on pages 111–112. Plan your flower observation log. Then answer the questions below on a sheet of paper. They will help you plan other details to write in the log.

1. What are you observing?

2. Where are you observing?

3. When are you observing?

4. What do you see? Write two details.

5. Which other senses can you use to tell about the flower?

6. What are some exact words that you could use in the log?

WRITE AWAY

You have been prewriting an observation log. On a sheet of paper, follow the other four steps in the writing process to complete the log. Don't forget to include a picture of the flower and its labels.

Opinion Paragraph

People often have different opinions, or feelings, about things. An **opinion paragraph** tells how a writer feels about something. It includes facts and details to support the opinion.

Here are some hints that will help you write an opinion paragraph.

- Write a topic sentence that clearly tells your opinion.

- Include facts, examples, and reasons that support your opinion.

- Add details that will help readers understand your opinion.

- Use linking words such as <u>because</u>, <u>and</u>, and <u>also</u> to connect ideas and organize your paragraph.

- Write an ending sentence that repeats your opinion using different words.

Here is an opinion paragraph.

I think everyone should learn how to swim. Swimming is fun, and it keeps you cool in hot weather. It is also a popular sport. If you know how to swim, you can join a swim team. This is a good way to meet people and stay active. The most important reason to learn how to swim is that it might save your life! If you don't know how to swim, it's time to learn.

Opinion Paragraph, part 2

Answer the questions on a sheet of paper.

1. What opinion do you want to write about?

2. What are some reasons why you have this opinion?

Use the Prewriting Survey on pages 111–112. Plan your opinion paragraph. Then answer the questions below on a sheet of paper. They will help you plan other details to write in the paragraph.

1. What is the fact that supports your opinion?

2. What is an example that supports your opinion?

3. What details can you use to make your opinion clearer?

4. What linking words can help you connect your ideas?

5. How can you tell your opinion differently in an ending sentence?

WRITE AWAY

You have been prewriting ideas for an opinion paragraph. Now follow the rest of the steps in the writing process. Review the steps on page 16 for publishing on the computer. Publish your opinion paragraph as part of a class blog. Be sure to check the comments to see if others agree with your opinion.

Book Report

A **book report** tells the main idea of a book. It also tells what you think about the book. However, a book report does not tell the ending.

Here are some hints that will help you write a book report.

- Tell the title of the book in the topic sentence. Underline it.
- Write the author's name.
- Tell the main idea of the book.
- Tell something interesting from the book.
- Tell what you think about the book.

Here is a book report.

I read a book called <u>The Koalas</u>. Anita Best wrote it. The book gives lots of facts about koalas. I found out that koalas live in Australia. They live in trees and eat leaves. I think this is a good book because it tells great things about koalas.

Answer the questions.

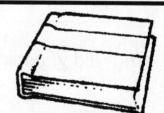

1. What book would you like to tell about?

_____

2. Why do you want to tell about this book?

_____

Name _____ Date _____

Book Report, part 2

Use the Prewriting Survey on pages 111–112
to plan your book report. Then answer the
questions below. They will help you write a
great book report.

1. Who wrote the book? _____

2. Is the book real or make-believe? How do you know?

   _____

3. What is the main idea of the book? _____

   _____

4. If the book is make-believe, who is in the story? _____

5. If the book is make-believe, where does it take place? _____

6. If the book is real, what is an important detail? _____

   _____

7. What did you think about the book? _____

   _____

WRITE AWAY

You have been prewriting ideas for a book report. Review the hints on
page 99. Then follow the rest of the steps in the writing process. You
might want to publish your book report on a computer. Review the steps
on page 16 for ideas.

Unit 4
Core Skills Writing, Grade 2

Short Story

A **short story** is fun to read and write. It entertains the reader. It has **characters** that have a problem to fix. The characters are the people and animals in the story. All stories have a beginning, a middle, and an end.

Here are some hints to help you write a story.

- Write the beginning. Tell the names of the characters. Tell where and when the story takes place.

- Write the middle. Tell what the problem is. Tell what the characters do to fix the problem. Tell about the characters' thoughts and feelings. Put the events in time order.

- Write the ending. Tell how the characters fix the problem.

- Give the story a title. Underline it.

Some favorite stories are <u>The Three Bears</u> and <u>Cinderella</u>.

Look at the picture. Then answer the questions on a sheet of paper. The questions will help you write a story.

1. Who are the main characters? Give them names.

2. Where and when does the story take place?

3. What is the problem?

Short Story, part 2

Use the Prewriting Survey on pages 111–112 to plan your short story. Then complete the chart below. It will help you write a story.

Beginning

Who is in the story? _____

Where does the story take place? _____

_____

When does the story take place? _____

What is the problem? _____

Middle

What happens in the story? List three story events in order.

Event 1 _____

Event 2 _____

Event 3 _____

What do the characters think? How do they feel?

Character 1 _____

Character 2 _____

Ending

How is the problem fixed? _____

_____

_____

Short Story, part 3

Look back at The Reader's Senses on page 36 and Words That Paint a Picture on page 37. Think about how you might use sense words and paint word pictures in your story. Then answer the questions below.

1. What words can help the reader know how each character looks and sounds?

   a. Character 1 _____

   b. Character 2 _____

2. What words can help the reader know how each character feels?

   a. Character 1 _____

   b. Character 2 _____

3. What words can help the reader know about where and when the story takes place?

   a. How does the place look? _____

   b. What sounds can you hear? _____

   c. How does the place smell? _____

4. Now think about the story events. List some words that might help you describe these events.

   _____

   _____

   _____

Short Story, part 4

Think about more ways to bring your story to life for a reader. Use the questions below to help with ideas.

1. What words can show what each character is thinking?

   _____

2. Will your characters speak? What will they say?

   _____

3. Which action words can show what happens in the story?

   _____

4. Which time-order words can show the order of events?

   _____

5. What ideas will you put in the story ending?

   _____

WRITE AWAY

You have been prewriting ideas for a short story. Review the hints on page 101. Then follow the steps in the writing process. With your teacher's help, publish your story as part of a class blog. Review page 16 for ideas.

Research Report

> A **research report** gives information about a topic in the writer's own words.
>
> Here are some hints to help you write a research report.
>
> - Write an introduction that tells the main idea, or what the report is about.
> - In the body of the report, give interesting facts and details about the main idea.
> - Add pictures, charts, or graphs about your main idea.
> - Write a conclusion that sums up ideas in your report.

Follow the directions below.

I. Think of topics that interest you. Write a list of topics you like.

_____

_____

_____

_____

_____

2. Choose a topic from the list for your research report. Make sure you choose just one thing. For example, there are many, many kinds of wild animals. "Wild animals" would not be a good topic. Instead, choose just one wild animal for your report.

Research Report, part 2

Questions are a starting point for your research report. First you will write questions. Then you will look for answers to your questions.

Here are some sample questions.

- Where do tigers live? What do tigers eat? Do all tigers have stripes?

- What do bears eat? Do all bears live in the woods? Do bears sleep all winter?

- Do all lions have manes? Do lions live alone or in groups? Where do lions live?

Now it is time to look for answers to your questions. You can look for answers in the library. You can also look for answers on the Internet.

Some library sources you can use are books and reference books, magazines and newspapers, CDs and DVDs, and videos.

Write three questions about your topic below.

_____

_____

_____

Your teacher or librarian can help you find good sites on the Internet. Look on those sites for answers to your questions.

Research Report, part 3

You will find a lot of facts and details during your research. How will you remember it all? A good way is to **take notes** while you read. Here are things to write on your note cards.

- The question you want to answer, or a main idea
- Details and key words
- Direct quote
- Information about the source

Your note cards might look like these.

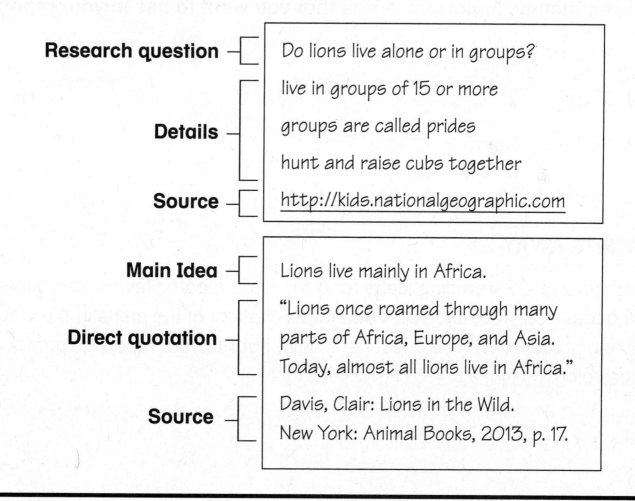

Research question — Do lions live alone or in groups?

Details —
live in groups of 15 or more
groups are called prides
hunt and raise cubs together

Source — http://kids.nationalgeographic.com

Main Idea — Lions live mainly in Africa.

Direct quotation — "Lions once roamed through many parts of Africa, Europe, and Asia. Today, almost all lions live in Africa."

Source — Davis, Clair: Lions in the Wild. New York: Animal Books, 2013, p. 17.

107

Research Report, part 4

> You are almost ready to write your research report. Remember that your report will have these parts.
>
> - An introduction that tells what the report is about
> - A body that has facts and details about your topic
> - Pictures, graphs, or charts
> - An ending that sums up what is in the report

Write ideas for the parts of your research report on a sheet of paper. Include important words that you want to use in your report.

1. Introduction

2. Body

3. Pictures, Graphs, or Charts

4. Ending

WRITE AWAY

You have been prewriting ideas for a research report. Review your notes on pages 105, 106, and 107. Then follow the rest of the steps in the writing process. With your teacher's help, publish your report as part of a class blog.

Name _____ Date _____

Journal Paper

Date _____

Dear Journal,

_____

_____

_____

_____

_____

_____

Name _____ Date _____

The Writing Process

There are five steps in the writing process.

Prewriting

• Plan what you will write.

• List your ideas or make a web.

• Think about who will read the work.

• Think about what writing form to use.

Drafting

• Put your ideas into words and sentences.

• Don't worry about mistakes. You will fix them later!

Revising

• Make sure your ideas are easy to understand.

• Add or remove details so the writing makes sense.

• Put the sentences in order.

• Choose exact words and use sense words.

• Join sentences.

• Use long sentences and short sentences.

• Begin sentences with different words.

• Make a clean copy of your work.

Blackline Masters
Core Skills Writing, Grade 2

The Writing Process, part 2

Proofreading

- Read once to make sure that words beginning with a capital letter are correct.

- Read a second time to make sure all the end marks and commas are correct.

- Read a third time to make sure all of the words are spelled correctly.

Publishing

- Make a clean copy.

- Draw a picture.

- Choose a title.

- Make a cover if you wish.

- Share your work!

Prewriting Survey

My Purpose

1. What am I writing about?

   _____

2. What do I want to say?

   _____

3. What is my purpose for writing? Explain.

   _____

   _____

My Audience

4. Who will be reading my writing?

   _____

5. What new information will I tell my audience?

   _____

Writing Pattern

6. Which writing pattern would best help my audience understand the topic? Circle one.

   Main idea and details   Sequence of events   Compare and contrast

   Problem and solution   Cause and effect   Summary

Name _____   Date _____

Prewriting Survey, part 2

Planning

7. Which graphic organizer can help me plan the details of my writing? Circle all the ones that you could use.

Main idea and details web   Sequence chart   Venn diagram

Problem and solution chart   Cause and effect chart   Summary chart

Writing Purpose and Details

8. Why am I writing? (Choose one purpose below and write the details you want to share.)

To inform (To give facts about a topic)	Who What Where When Why How
To express (To share a feeling or idea)	What I see What I hear What I touch What I smell What I taste
To entertain (To tell a story)	
To persuade (To make a reader feel or think a certain way)	

Prewriting Survey, part 3

Writing Form

9. What will my final form be? (Circle one.)

Play	Poem	Rhyme	Poster
Report	Short Story	Journal	Letter
Observation Log	Song	True Story	Biography
Personal Narrative	Book Report	Description	Opinion
How-to Paragraph	Other _____		

Proofreading Checklist

Use the list to check your writing for mistakes.

Capitalization

☐ Do all sentences begin with a capital letter?

☐ Do all titles and special names begin with a capital letter?

☐ Do all place names begin with a capital letter?

☐ Do all months and days begin with a capital letter?

Punctuation

☐ Does each sentence have an end mark (period, question mark, exclamation mark)?

☐ Does a comma separate items in a list?

☐ Is a comma correctly used with dates and addresses?

☐ Are quotation marks used around the words that people say?

☐ Does an apostrophe show when something belongs to someone?

Spelling

☐ Are all the words spelled correctly?

☐ Did I use a dictionary to check words I think may not be spelled correctly?

☐ Did I use a dictionary to check troublesome words?

Proofreading Marks

Use the marks to proofread your writing.

≡ Use a capital letter.

/ Use a lowercase letter.

⊙ Add a period.

∧ Add something.

⤷ Take out something.

⋏ Change something.

◯ Check the spelling.

Name _____ Date _____

Writing Traits Checklist

Title _____

Trait	Strong	Average	Needs Improvement
Ideas			
Tell about one important idea. It is the main idea.			
Choose a main idea that is interesting.			
Add details. Details are the facts that tell more about your main idea.			
Details should tell what you see, hear, smell, taste, and feel.			
Organization			
Choose a writing form that makes the information clear. (Letters, e-mail messages, stories, and journals are some writing forms that you can choose.)			
Show a beginning, a middle, and an end.			
Write the first sentence so that it catches the reader's interest.			
Put details in order.			
Use time-order words to show the order. (first, next, then, finally, after that, at the same time)			
Voice			
Choose words that show your feelings.			
Choose words that your reader can understand.			
Words			
Choose words that help a reader see, hear, taste, smell, and touch.			
Use strong action words to tell what is happening.			
Use exact words.			
Use new words.			

Writing Traits Checklist, part 2

Trait	Strong	Average	Needs Improvement
Sentences			
Write sentences that are short and long.			
Write sentences that begin with different kinds of words.			
Write sentences that sound like someone is talking.			
Proofreading			
Write from left to right.			
Put a space between all words.			
Write a capital letter at the beginning of each sentence.			
Write an end mark at the end of each sentence.			
Write a capital letter at the beginning of each special noun.			
Write a comma in a date and list of items.			
Spell all words correctly.			
Sharing			
Write an interesting title.			
Draw pictures to show the main ideas.			
Make the final copy clean and neat.			
Make a cover.			

Writing Interest Survey

1. How often do you like to read? Check one.

☐ often   ☐ not often

☐ sometimes   ☐ never

2. What is your favorite book? Why?

_____

_____

3. What do you like to read? Check as many as you want.

☐ newspapers   ☐ magazines   ☐ biography   ☐ poetry

☐ science fiction   ☐ adventure   ☐ fantasy   ☐ mystery

☐ historical fiction   ☐ humor   ☐ realistic fiction

☐ nonfiction (What kinds?) _____

☐ other _____

4. What would you like to do better as a reader?

☐ understand what I read   ☐ read faster

☐ read harder books   ☐ other _____

5. When you write, how do you like to work?

☐ in a large group   ☐ in pairs

☐ in a small group   ☐ alone

Writing Interest Survey, part 2

6. How often do you like to write? Check one.

☐ less than once a week

☐ I or 2 times per week

☐ 3 or 4 times per week

☐ every day (7 times a week)

7. What kinds of writing do you like to do? Check as many as you want.

☐ true stories   ☐ letters   ☐ poems   ☐ journal or diary

☐ reports   ☐ articles   ☐ songs   ☐ research papers

☐ make-believe stories ☐ real stories   ☐ riddles   ☐ mysteries

☐ other _____

8. What do you like most about writing? _____

_____

_____

9. What do you like least about writing? _____

_____

_____

Main Idea and Details Web

Write the main idea in the oval. Write four good details in the circles.

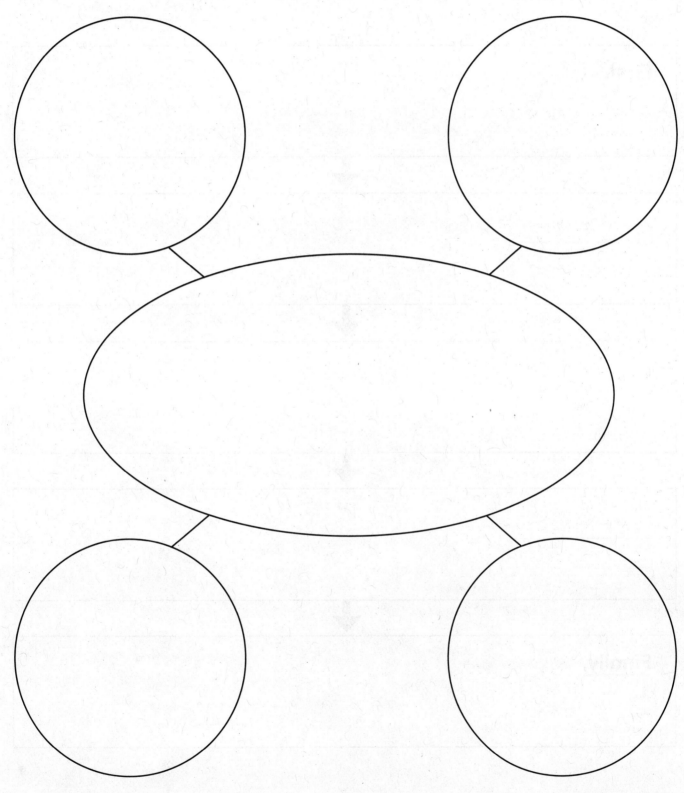

Name _____   Date _____

Sequence Chart

Write the steps or events in the order that they happen. Write time-order words on the lines to help you explain the order.

<u>First,</u>

_____,

_____,

_____,

<u>Finally,</u>

122

Name _____ Date _____

Venn Diagram

Write the names of the things you are comparing on the lines above the circles. In the overlapping space, tell how the things are the same. In the rest of the circle, tell how each thing is different.

A _____   B _____

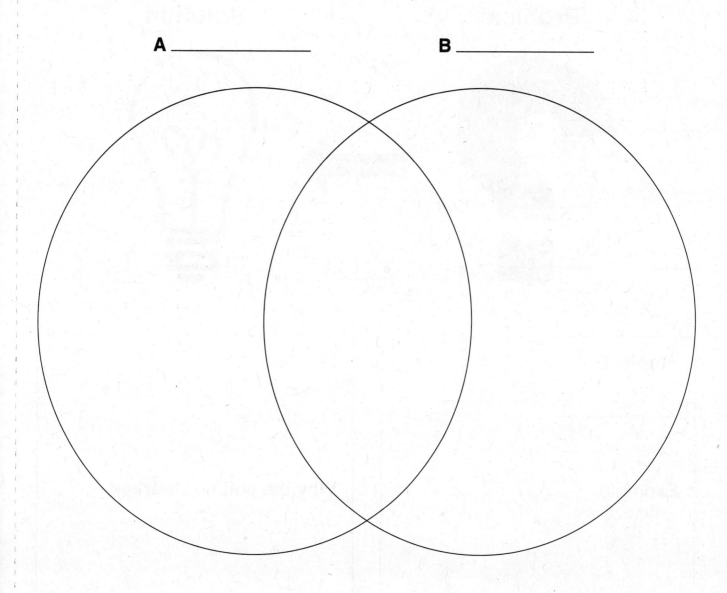

123

Problem and Solution Chart

Write the problem in the box below the question mark. Complete the box. Then write the solution in the box below the light bulb. Complete that box, too.

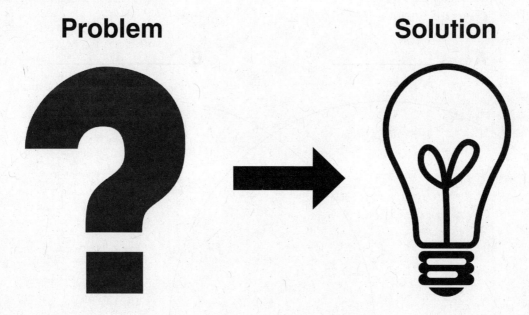

Problem	Solution

Problem

Example

Details

Solution

Why the solution worked

Cause and Effect Charts

Write what happened in the Effect box. Write the reason it happened in the Cause box.

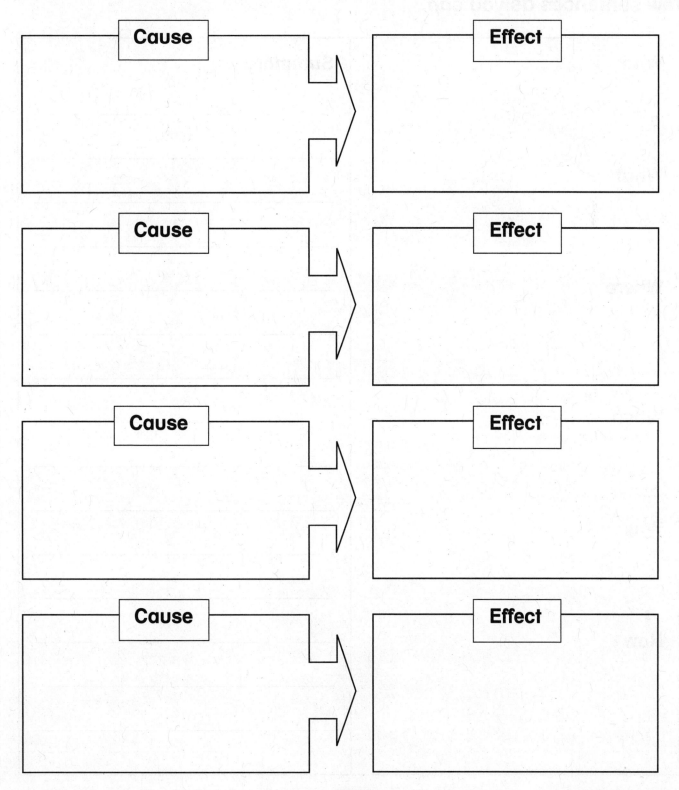

Summary Chart

Write the details on the left side of the chart. Write a summary on the right side of the chart. Try to include all the information in as few sentences as you can.

Who	Summary
	_____
	_____
What	_____
	_____
Where	_____
	_____
	_____
When	_____
	_____
Why	_____
	_____
	_____
How	_____
	_____
	_____

Answer Key

Student answers will vary on the pages not included in this Answer Key. Accept all reasonable answers.

Page 1
1. words
2. think
3. clearly

Page 4
Possible answers are given.
1. D
2. C
3. D
4. B

Page 5
1. adult
2. child
3. teen

Page 6
1. thing
2. place
3. person

Page 8
Possible answers are given.
1. chair, it
2. boys, they
3. girl, she

Page 9
1. read
2. run
3. jump

Page 10
1. The children play a game.
2. The children played a game yesterday.

Page 15
Hoppy the Frog did not like to hop. He liked to run. then one day, Slide the Snake got close to Hoppy. Hoppy ran, but slide stayed right beside him. Then, Hoppy hopped. Slide culd could not hop. Hoppy got away ⊙ Hoppy decided that he liked to hop after all!

Page 17
1. A boy builds a snowman.
2. Accept reasonable answers.

Page 18
Order: 3, 2, 1

Page 22
Elton has a dog named rolo. Elton took Rolo to the park ⊙ Rolo chased a squirrel. He chased a burd bird . he did not chase the stick that Elton threw. By then, Rolo was too tired!

Page 25
1. no
2. yes
3. yes
4. yes
5. no

Page 26
Answers may vary.
1. It is fall.
2. The leaves are falling.
3. Anna rakes the leaves.
4. She is having fun.

Page 29
1. Ann went to the park.
2. Sara came with her.
3. They ran to the swings.

Page 37
1. Children should underline José and the wind. Both are fast.
2. Children should underline Max's heart and a drum. Both beat loudly.
3. Children should underline the building and a giant. Both are very tall.

Page 38
Possible answers are given.
1. large
2. small
3. angry
4. raced

Page 39
1. clean
2. dry
3. cold
4. opened

Page 40
1. to
2. buy
3. red
4. four

Page 41
1. Hippo found a ball and got an umbrella.
2. He put them in the car and drove to the beach.
3. The ocean water felt cool and tasted salty.

Page 42
1. Jan and Alex worked in the garden.
2. Fruits and vegetables grew in it.
3. A butterfly and a bee flew into their garden.

Page 43
1. Mr. West cooked fish, beans, and peas.
2. Jill, Kim, and Ron bought milk.
3. Mrs. Luna bought eggs, cheese, and yogurt.

Page 46
Possible answers are given.
1. Pat got out a paintbrush. He got paints, too.
2. He looked for paper. Pat could not find it.
3. Pat went to the store, and he bought paper.

Page 47
1. Greg went to the park on friday ⊙
2. he took a kite.
3. Greg had fun fling flying the kite ⊙

© Houghton Mifflin Harcourt Publishing Company

Answer Key
Core Skills Writing, Grade 2

Page 50

1. A frog has strong, long back legs.
2. Children should write two of the remaining four sentences.

Page 51

1. Children should underline *Rita bought a ball for her cat.*
2. Children should number the sentences as follows:
   1. The ball is blue.
   2. It has a bell inside.
   3. Rita rolls the ball on the floor.
   4. Her cat chases it.
3. Children should circle *Rita's cat likes to play with the ball.*

Page 52

Order: 4, 2, 5, 1, 3

Page 60

Order: 1, 5, X, 3, 4, 2

Page 61

The most likely answer is given.

Jason was playing with his little red robot. He made the robot go left. He **also** made the robot go right. Jason made it roll under the chair, **too.** He laughed when his cat flew out from under the chair. The cat did not like playing with the little red robot.

Page 62

One possible answer is given.

Making a peanut butter sandwich is easy. **First,** you spread peanut butter on one slice of bread. **Then,** you spread jelly on top of the peanut butter. **Next,** you place another slice of bread on the jelly. Yum! **Finally,** you can eat the peanut butter and jelly sandwich.